MOMENTS THAT BECAME MEMORIES

BILLY COLEMAN JONES

TABLE OF CONTENTS

The Comforting Arms Of My Loving Father 13

Smokey's Home At Last 17

Who Is This Strange Acting Woman? 21

The Faith Of A Four Year Old Little Girl.........................24

How I Met And Married My Sweetheart 30

My First Home Cooked Meal 38

God's Special Gift To Us 43

Song Lyrics "Angel's Song" 50

A Fishing Trip I Will Never Forget.....................53

The One And Only Time I Ever Went Frog Gigging.........59

A Coke Bottle, Fishing Line And Spam...........................62

My Special Brother 68

A Lesson I Had To Learn The Hard Way 79

Song Lyrics "Wednesday Night Prayer Meeting" 88

The Saddest But Happiest Day Of My Life......................91

Song Lyrics "How Did Peter Get Back To The Boat?"....107

My Stepmother, Frances Parrish Jones 110

Song Lyrics "Called To Be Faithful" 116

The Day Our Lives Changed Forever..............................118

No! This Cannot Be Happening To Me 128

That's Just The Way He Is 137

My Dad, Rev. Willie Bennett Jones (Billy Jones) 143

In Loving Memory Of My Mom, "Anna Oakes Jones" ..155

INTRODUCTION

Well, here we go! I have no idea how this is going to turn out, but it's something I've thought about doing for quite some time. I've wanted to write a collection of short stories about some precious, unforgettable, funny and even sad moments in my life. For one reason or another, these moments have remained fresh in my memory, as if they happened just yesterday. Even now when I think about them, some make me laugh and some bring tears to my eyes and some . . . well, "What can I say?" They're just precious, but when you boil it all down, isn't that what life is really about? ~ **MOMENTS THAT BECAME MEMORIES**

DEDICATION

I want to dedicate this book to my wife, Louise. Thank you for putting up with me and loving me even when I was undeserving of your love. I'm so thankful for what we have in each other. This road we've been traveling for the past 42 years has not always been an easy road, but I wouldn't trade it for anything. I'd rather be poor with you than to be rich without you. I love you more than you will ever know. Thank you for making my life complete and for being a part of this collection of precious, unforgettable, funny and yes, sometimes even sad moments that we call, "Memories".

ACKNOWLEDGEMENTS

So many people have influenced my life. Having been a preacher's son I've lived in many different places. Therefore, I have made a lot of friends who are still precious to me though I don't see them often. Many of them are mentioned in my book, but there are so many more.

I want to especially acknowledge my church family at the Swansonville Pentecostal Holiness Church where I have attended for the past twenty-seven years. You are precious and dear people to me. Thank you for your love and support to me and my family.

I come from a very large family. I'm the oldest of thirty grandchildren just on my dad's side and there are eleven grandchildren on my mom's side. I'll never forget those times we were together as we were growing up. You all are so dear to me. I love and appreciate every one of you.

I want to acknowledge one special person and that's my fishing buddy, Wayland Loftin. Wayland, I cherish your friendship and thank you for the moments we've spent in the boat that have become memories.

Thank you all for being in my life and for being a part of those "Moments That Became Memories."

THE COMFORTING ARMS
OF MY LOVING FATHER

I n 1952 my Dad graduated from Holmes Bible College in Greenville, S.C. and took his first church as pastor of the Bethel Pentecostal Holiness Church in Gladys, Virginia. Even though I was only four and a half years old I still remember moving there. So many sights and sounds from those years are etched forever in my memory. Sounds such as that bucket hitting the water at the bottom of the well when my Mom would draw water, or the blood curdling scream coming from the outhouse when my Mom looked down and saw a black snake curled up around her feet. The sight of that door flying open and her trying to run with her panties around her ankles still makes me laugh even now. I remember Dad's first two converts as pastor of the Bethel church, Junior and Lorene Mitchell. They had a little red headed freckle faced girl named Brenda who became my very first girlfriend at the ripe old age of six. My wife and I are still very close friends with Brenda and her husband Lynn. I could go on and on, but there is one memory from Bethel that is especially precious and dear to me.

I don't remember if the church already had that old bus or if they bought it after we moved there, but Dad would jump in that old thing, go out and pick up people and bring them to church. Later on after Junior Mitchell got saved, he and Dad would take turns driving. I loved riding that old bus because all of us kids would sit in the back and play.

I remember one particular Sunday night when Daddy was to drive the bus. After the service was over everybody went their separate ways, some in their cars and some on the church bus. Mom had taken my two little brothers, Byron and Harold, and gone home as usual. Dad thought I had gone home with Mom and Mom thought I was with Dad, but I had fallen asleep on a church pew. I'll never forget waking up in the dark and when I say dark, I mean DARK! You couldn't see your hand in front of your face. We were way out in the country and there were no street lights. I was so scared. I remember screaming and crying, "Daddy, Daddy" but there was no answer. I tried to remember which pew I was laying on so maybe I could find my way to the door.

I remember bumping into everything. I mean it was complete, T-total darkness and I was one scared five year-old little boy. I finally found the front door, but it was locked. I don't remember how long I stood there, but it seemed like a lifetime. All of a sudden I heard something! Way off in the distance I heard the sound of an old church bus. Nobody will ever know how beautiful that sound was to that five year-old little boy. I listened as it pulled into the yard. When the motor shut off I started screaming "Daddy, Daddy" but he couldn't hear me. When Daddy went in the house Mama asked him where I was. He said, "I thought he was with you." Mama said, "I thought he was with you." All of a sudden I heard the sound of footsteps running to the church, then I saw the flashlight shining under the door and then I heard the sound of keys. When the door finally opened my Daddy grabbed me up in his arms and said "Son, I'm so sorry." I had cried for so long I had what the old folks used to call the snubs.

I don't remember how long he knelt there and held me but I do know this, I didn't have to walk home, he carried me. It was then I knew everything was going to be alright because my Daddy kept telling me it was. What I felt at that moment in the arms of my loving father made it all worthwhile.

Well, there have been other times in my life when I was lost in the dark and I couldn't find my way. It was at that very moment when I cried out to my heavenly father I felt His loving arms slip around me and I knew, just as before, everything was going to be alright! I thank God every day for, "THE COMFORTING ARMS OF MY LOVING FATHER." Both of my fathers!

SMOKEY'S HOME AT LAST

I will never forget the first time I saw Smokey. He was the cutest ball of fur you ever saw. A six week old registered German Shepherd puppy that I fell in love with as soon as I laid eyes on him. From day one Smokey and I were best friends. He wanted to go with me everywhere. When he was a puppy he was solid black, but as he got older his eyebrows and his chest started turning silver. He was a beautiful dog, but more than that he was my buddy!

When Smokey was about four years old I came home from work one day and he was nowhere to be found. I walked to all the places we enjoyed going to, such as the pond, where I would throw a stick into the water and he would swim out, get it and bring it back to me so I could throw it again. He wasn't there. Every afternoon after I got home from work, I would drive up and down the roads within a few miles of our home looking for him, but I couldn't find him anywhere. Some days I yelled his name over and over and over until I was just about hoarse. I went to the dog pound, but he wasn't there. After about three or four weeks of searching, my wife Louise said, "Honey it's time to let go." I knew she was right, but I didn't want to let go. It was like giving up on my buddy. I still searched for him, but as time passed I lost hope and finally stopped looking. You'll never know the times we would be driving to the store or to work or just anywhere, and out of the corner of my eye I thought I saw him, only to be disappointed.

One afternoon about eight months later, I was a quarter of a mile or so from home and I could see Louise in the front yard. I couldn't tell exactly what she was doing from that distance, but she appeared to be talking to someone or something. Suddenly, I saw what it was . . . a black and silver German Shepherd. I quickly pulled into the driveway, slid to a stop, jumped out of the car and stared in total disbelief. She said, "Can you believe this? After all this time he's come home." I could tell by the expression on her face she was so pleased that she had found my buddy for me. As soon as he saw me he came running and jumped up on me. I said, "Where in the world did you find him?" She said, "He was about a mile up the road in somebody's front yard. I bet they've had him this whole time and he got away." I asked, "How did you get him home?" She replied, "Our neighbor, Mr. Compton, was coming down the road in his pickup truck and I flagged him down. As soon as he opened the tailgate Smokey jumped right in. Mr. Compton brought him home for me."

I kept hugging Smokey and he was licking my face, but I wasn't totally convinced yet. Although he acted like he was glad to see me something just didn't seem right. I said, "His color seems lighter than it used to be and he seems smaller." She said, "A dog's color will change over a period of time. You've got to remember he's been gone eight months." About that time Smokey rolled over on his back. I started scratching his belly like I had always done and it was at that moment I knew. I said, "Honey, you're right, over a period of time a dog's color can change, but it doesn't matter how much time goes by, a male dog will not turn into a female."

Seldom in my life have I witnessed the degree of disappointment I saw on her face. She thought she had given my best friend back to me that day. Though she didn't know it at the time, she gave me something much more precious than that. She gave me the assurance, once again, that she really and truly loved me and cared about my hurts and my disappointments. She thought she had done something to really make me happy. Well honey, all I can say is, "Mission accomplished!"

WHO IS THIS STRANGE ACTING WOMAN?

WARNING: Do not attempt this at home or anywhere else. It could be hazardous to your health and possibly end your life. Now, I feel better about telling this story having preceded it with this warning.

This particular day was no different from any other workday. We got up, went to work and we came home, nothing eventful at all, at least not to this point. As usual Louise unlocked the front door and went in while I went to the mailbox. When I got to the house she had taken her shoes off and was reclined on the couch. I laid the mail on the coffee table and sat down on the love seat. Louise reached for the Reader's Digest while I looked through the bills. When I had finished I laid the mail back on the coffee table and picked up the brown wrapper Louise had placed there, you know, the one the Reader's Digest always comes wrapped in? It had a sweepstakes entry form attached to it and as I pulled the sweepstakes entry form from the wrapper I noticed it was attached by a strip of silicone glue that was about three inches long. It was clear and very sticky. I proceeded to carefully peel it from the wrapper and it was at that moment the "idea" hit me. Now, you can call it creative genius, meanness or whatever term you want to use, but I definitely wouldn't use the word "inspired." I took a deep breath and let out one of the loudest fake sneezes you've ever heard in your life and immediately stuck that thing right on the end of my nose. I held my head forward so it would dangle out in front of me. It looked like the real thing. When Louise looked up you should have seen her face. "OH GROSS get a tissue quick it's going to drop on the love seat!" I just sat there and let it swing. The longer I sat the louder she got. "DO SOMETHING QUICK!" So I did. I reached up, pulled it off my nose and started slinging it as if I were trying to get it off my finger. When I let go it landed on her. Folks, at that moment I saw a side of my wife I'd never seen before. She began to levitate about a foot off the couch, at least it seemed that way to me. She showed a very un-Christ like spirit. You wouldn't believe the tone of voice she used and, oooh the things she said to me. Although I will say in her defense, she never once used any bad words. She said, "Have you completely lost what little bit of sense you ever had? I believe that sneeze did something to your brain!" To make matters worse I was laughing so hard I couldn't speak and that made her even madder. "Get something and get this snot off me. I can't believe you did that." Finally, I reached over, picked it up and held it up so she could see what it was. When she finally started laughing I knew I was safe. That was one of my proudest moments. I got her good.

Now, normally I try to write something sweet and inspirational at the end of each story, but to be honest with you, I can't think of a thing to say except, I'm just glad I'm still here!

THE FAITH OF A FOUR
YEAR OLD LITTLE GIRL

*God can speak to us in so many ways if we will just stop
and listen. He can take an event from one single day and
speak volumes to us. That's exactly what He did for me on
this particular day.*

"Hey girls, let's get ready and go to the new IHOP for breakfast." It was Saturday morning, the day before Easter Sunday. We had slept in for a little while but that was pretty much a normal thing on Saturdays. The new IHOP in Danville, Virginia had only been open a few weeks. Our daughter, Angel, was about four years old at that time, but she had already come to the conclusion that most all members of the female gender come to at one time or another. She loved to go out to eat. Up to that point we were all moving kind of slow that morning, but upon hearing my suggestion, things livened up quickly and it wasn't long before the Joneses were on their way to IHOP for breakfast.

As we walked through the entrance at IHOP we noticed there were pictures everywhere. They had been colored by kids who had eaten at the restaurant over the previous week or two. The name and age of each child was written on the front of their picture. There must have been hundreds of them taped to the walls. We noticed that something else had captured Angel's attention though. On one of the seats where customers normally sit while waiting for a table, were two very large Easter baskets and two large stuffed Easter bunnies. I believe they were the largest I've ever seen. Angel stood there with a big smile and just gazed at them. The hostess told us they were having a coloring contest for Easter and the larger basket and bunny were going to the first place winner and the smaller ones were going to the second place winner.

There was a line of customers ahead of us so it took a few minutes to get a table. After being seated we placed our order and while waiting for our food the waitress brought a picture and a box of crayons to our table and asked if Angel would like to color a picture for the contest. I'm sure you already know what her answer was. I can still see her now with her little tongue sticking out the corner of her mouth as she worked on her picture. You should have seen her little face. Yeah, I know what you're thinking, but I can't help it, she looked like a little doll. For the next hour that picture received her undivided attention.

Louise and I finished our breakfast but Angel had not touched hers at all. I don't know how many times I told her to hurry up and eat, but I don't think she even heard me. It was like talking to a brick wall and I must say, even now fourteen years later, that part hasn't changed one bit. "Angel, you've got to eat. Your food is getting cold and we've got a lot of places to go, so please hurry up baby." I can hear her response now, "OK Daddy, I'm almost finished." Finally she said, "I'm all done Daddy. Do you want to see it?" I replied, "It's beautiful baby, but we've got to go." I must say though, she really did a good job.

I knew we had a problem on our hands because all she talked about the rest of the day was her Easter basket and bunny rabbit. I didn't want to discourage her, but at the same time I didn't want her to be hurt and disappointed. I guess that's part of being a Daddy. We want to protect our children from the disappointments that life can and will bring.

For the rest of that day all we heard were things like, "Wonder when they are going to call me?" Or, "Mom, I'm going to sleep with my big bunny rabbit, OK?" I kept saying things such as, "Forget about that sweetheart, you did a good job, but listen to Daddy, there were hundreds of pictures on that wall so you just be proud of the job you did and don't worry about it." Yeah right, like that was really going to end it.

We finally finished all our errands which took most of the day and then headed for home. When we got there I checked the answering machine as usual. There were several messages, but I'll never forget the one that said, "Mr. Jones, this is the manager at IHOP. When you come in would you please give me a call? I'll be here until 10:00 tonight." I called the number he had left and asked for the manager. When I told him who I was he said, "Mr. Jones, how soon can you be here? Your daughter, Angel, won a prize and we would like to take some pictures of her." The first thing that came to my mind was, they're giving something to all the kids who participated. I asked "What did she win?" When he said, "First Place" I almost dropped the phone. I told him we would leave right away.

When I yelled out, "Angel, do you want to go to IHOP and get your big Easter basket and bunny rabbit?" Louise ran into the room and said, "Don't you tease her like that. You're going to hurt her feelings. I can't believe you would do that to her! That's not funny!" I said, "Honey, calm down. They called . . . she won first place!" I didn't think she really believed me so I replayed the message that he had left.

You should have seen Angel smiling for those pictures. It was that same smile we had seen since she first laid eyes on that big bunny rabbit.

You know, according to my Bible that's the kind of faith it's going to take for us to make it to heaven.

Matthew 18:2-3

*And Jesus called a little child unto him, and set him in the midst of them, and said, **"Verily I say unto you, Except ye be converted, and become as little children, ye shall not enter into the kingdom of heaven."***

My prayer is, "God, birth within me that childlike faith I saw in my little girl that day."

Billy & Louise
October 12, 1969

HOW I MET AND MARRIED
MY SWEETHEART

I met Louise at a church youth camp in the summer of 1967 at the Western North Carolina Conference Headquarters of the Pentecostal Holiness Church in Greensboro, North Carolina. I was 19 and she was 16. Actually, I was not a camper. Someone had invited me to go for an evening service to meet this girl from Newport News, Virginia named Louise

West. We were living in Gretna, Virginia at that time. I wasn't all that interested in going all the way to Greensboro, but it so happened that the lady who invited me had a brand new car. So I told her I would go if she would let me drive. Her niece and Louise were best friends so I figured, what could it hurt? At least I would get to drive a new car out of the deal. We met and went to church together that night. Rev. Hugh Hoyle was doing the preaching for youth camp and since I had won the talent contest for our conference they asked me to sing. I remember I was very nervous. Louise seemed to be a real sweet and nice girl. The fact that she was very pretty didn't hurt any either, but there was a problem. There was someone else I was interested in at the time. Louise and I wrote each other a few times, but since the girl I was interested in had become my girlfriend, I didn't write anymore.

In June of 1968 I was drafted into the Army. While stationed at Fort Ord, California my girlfriend decided she didn't want to wait for me, so that ended. Not long after that, Louise wrote to my brother requesting a copy of a gospel album we had recorded just before I went in the Army. When he sent it to her he also sent my address. Much to my surprise I got the sweetest letter from her and that was the beginning of the best thing that ever happened to me, that is besides the Lord. She wrote every day after that. Some days I got as many as three letters at one time. I wrote as much as duty would allow.

In December I flew home for Christmas and went to see her. We had not seen each other since we met at youth camp a year and a half earlier. I met her family and got to spend a few days with them. I'm a very sentimental person. Believe it or not, the shirt I wore the first time I went to see her is still hanging in my closet. It's 43 years old and I outgrew it over 40 years ago, but I still have it and I cannot bring myself to throw it away.

One afternoon Louise and I were at the park not far from her house. To this day I don't know what came over me but I looked at her and said, "I don't know when, but one day I'm going to marry you." She got the biggest laugh out of that but somehow I knew she was the one. After I returned to California we continued to write but that wasn't enough. We called just about every day and trust me calling from coast to coast was very expensive. Things were getting serious. In March I had some leave time built up so I flew home. We had been talking about getting married so we decided to make the announcement to her family. I'll never forget how nervous I was. Louise's sister, Annette, was the only one who knew about our plans to make the announcement, so along with help from their mother, who had no idea what was going on, they prepared a big evening meal. The plan was, sometime during the meal I would ask for everyone's attention and then make the announcement. I kept waiting for an opportunity but there wasn't one. There were eight people at the table and I couldn't get a word in. Louise's Dad was talking ninety miles an hour so finally Annette said, "Daddy, will you please be quiet for just a minute? Billy has something to say." Every eye at the table was focused on me. To make matters even worse Louise's old boyfriend was there. Now, how that happened I don't have a clue. All I know is I was scared to death. I don't remember exactly what I said or how I said it but it was something like, "Louise and I would like your permission to get married." Her Daddy jumped right in and said OK I'll sign the papers tonight, but her Mom had a different idea. She said, "If you'll wait until you're out of the Army it will be just fine." She was afraid if I went to Vietnam I might not come back and we understood how she felt. Our plans were to get married the following Christmas if I was still in the states.

I loved coming home, but going back was very difficult, and that time had arrived. It was so hard to say goodbye. It took about a week for me to get back into the swing of military life. Thank the Lord for all those letters from my Mom, Louise and everybody else who wrote. By the way, I still have every letter I received while I was in the Army. That's what kept me going. In one of Mom's letters she told me they were planning on driving to California on vacation and they were planning to bring Louise with them. The fact that my Mom and Dad, my eight year old sister Lynell, and my eleven month old baby brother David, (yes, I did say eleven month old baby brother) were all coming to see me was wonderful enough, but they were bringing my sweetheart.

Louise graduated from High School the first Sunday in June. That afternoon her Daddy and Granddaddy took her to my Mom and Dad's house in Gretna, Virginia. On Monday they left for California. During the week they spent with me we did a lot of sightseeing from San Diego to San Francisco. I believe that was one of the fastest weeks I've ever seen.

Once again we had to say goodbye. I remember standing there watching them drive away. I thought my heart would break, but I had to put up the front of being a tough soldier, which I was not. I had never been away from home until I went into the Army. That kind of lifestyle went against everything I had ever been taught. I saw and heard things that I had never seen or heard before in my life. I remember one day we were out in the field training. I don't remember exactly what happened but a Master Sergeant started cursing at me. Before I realized what I had done I said, "Sergeant, I've been taught all my life it's wrong to use that kind of language and I would appreciate it if you wouldn't use it to me." There was total silence as the Sergeant came running to me. He said, "Soldier, you get to my office right now. I'll be there in just a few minutes to take care of you." Needless to say I was literally scared to death. Those Sergeants were mean and enjoyed being that way. I was shaking all over as I sat there waiting for him. Finally, I heard him coming. As he burst through the door I stood to my feet and tried to brace myself for what was coming. When he got to me he held his hand out and said, "Soldier, I want to shake your hand. It took a man to do what you just did." You'll never know what a relief that was. I felt as though my death sentence had just been reprieved.

Well, a couple of months went by and one day I was called to the Battalion Headquarters. They wanted to know if I went to a certain building when I was transferred to the 54th M.P. Company. I told them this was the first time I had heard anything about it. I learned that when I finished my training, I was supposed to have been given papers to take there so my name would appear on the roster that was used for drawing personnel to be sent to Vietnam. My best friend, Ling Git Hsu, who was from Taiwan was with me. They said someone had made a mistake and since we had less than a year to serve we would be staying at Ft. Ord. You should have heard my Mom when I called her. It was shouting time in Gretna, Virginia. That was a direct answer to my Mother's prayers. She had been praying since June 26, 1968, the day I was drafted, that I wouldn't have to go to Vietnam.

Louise and I kept writing and calling, and calling, and calling, and finally we decided we could just about live on what we were spending on phone calls. I found out I could take three weeks leave the first of October so we moved our wedding date to October. Louise had a lot of work to do in a short period of time, but where there's a will there's a way.

Our special day finally arrived. Louise had done a beautiful job along with the help of her sister and others. On Sunday afternoon, October 12, 1969, at the Greenwood Pentecostal Holiness Church in Hampton, Virginia I watched my sweetheart walk down the aisle. She was beautiful!

Looking back over my life I can see where I've made some blunders. I've done some really dumb things along the way, but I can tell you this much, marrying Louise West was not one of them. We just celebrated our 41ˢᵗ anniversary and you know what? I really believe it's going to work out just fine. I thank God every day for my wife.

Proverbs 18: 22

***Whoso findeth a wife findeth a good thing, and
obtaineth favor of the Lord.***

MY FIRST HOME
COOKED MEAL

❧

O n Monday morning October 20, 1969, Louise and I
packed our car for the long trip from Gretna, Virginia
to Fort Ord, California. We had been married for a week and
a day and now it was time to get back to my military duties.
We left enough room for two skinny people to sit real close
in the front seat and that was it. The trunk, backseat and half
of the front seat of that 1969 Dodge were packed with all
of our earthly belongings. It's a good thing it was just the
two of us because there was no more room. We were just a
couple of dumb, excited, scared, happy and very broke kids
who loved each other very much.

We drove about eight to ten hours a day, although we did
set aside a little time to stop at the Grand Canyon and a few
other places of interest along the way. On Friday night at
about eight or nine o'clock, we finally pulled into our little

apartment in Marina, California, not far from Monterey. We were both exhausted from the trip but so glad to be there. Of course, the first thing we did was call our parents to let them know we had arrived safe and sound. We only took in what we had to have that night because we were so tired. When we laid down you wouldn't believe the noise that came from under the bed. We both jumped up to see what it was. Some of the young couples from the Marina Assembly of God Church, where I attended, had gone to our landlord and gotten a key. They went in and took the dust cover off the bottom of the box springs and filled it with anything that would make a noise. The next day they all came over to help us get moved in and to meet Louise. We didn't mention anything about what they had done and finally they asked how we liked the welcome home noise. They got a big laugh out of that. After we got everything in its place Louise said we needed to go to the grocery store. Setting up housekeeping for the first time meant buying everything which took quite a while, but we finally got it done and made it back home. After putting everything away, Louise said she was going to cook supper. That sounded good to me because I was getting hungry.

39

The very first home cooked meal after getting married is a very special event. You get a real good idea of what you may be facing the rest of your life. While in high school Louise was the first to get home so she would have supper ready when her Mom, Dad, sister and two brothers got there. She had always prepared for six people and so out of habit that's what she did on this occasion.

Now, I'm not the sharpest knife in the drawer, but I am sharp enough to know that when your new bride cooks your first meal you eat it all, ask for seconds and then brag about how good it was. I had never eaten what she fixed before, but it was really good. She took six pieces of tin foil and put a big chunk of hamburger on each one and then she cut up a potato on top of that. Next she added slices of onion and covered each one with Worcestershire sauce. The last thing she added was a healthy amount of garlic salt, which I had never eaten before. All kidding aside it was really good, especially that first one. The second one was pretty good, but that third one liked to have choked me. I didn't think I would ever get it down. She cooked six so I figured three for her and three for me. About an hour after we ate I started having really bad pains right in the middle of my chest. On a scale of one to ten with ten meaning call 911, I was at an 11. I said, "Honey, pray for me I'm hurting really bad." She started praying but it didn't help one bit. I thought to myself she can't pray any better than she can cook. (Not really, I just threw that in for fun.) Finally, I told her to go get Bill and Dwayla. Bill and Dwayla Patterson lived just a couple of apartments down from us. Bill was also in the Army and he was the Sunday School Superintendent at our church. They came up and laid hands on me and prayed, but it got worse. Finally, they put me in the car and rushed me to the hospital at Fort Ord. The doctors ran all kinds of tests and asked me what seemed like a million questions. During our conversation I mentioned that we were newly weds and my wife had cooked our first meal that night. After about two hours the doctors came in the room and they were all laughing. One of the doctors said, "I don't know if this is good news or not, but there's nothing wrong with your heart. You have acute indigestion," and handed me a big bottle of Maalox. They said it wasn't what I ate, but it was the amount I ate. The real culprit though, was the garlic salt. Louise was so embarrassed. She later said she thought she had married a man with a bad heart. I told her I thought I had married a woman who poisoned me for my military insurance.

This medical report was framed and hanging in our dining room, but for some reason Louise made me take it down. Over the past forty-one years we've laughed and told this story many, many times. It's just another one of those precious memories.

Angela Lynette Jones
Four Months Old

GOD'S SPECIAL GIFT TO US

S ix years after Louise and I got married we were living in Nashville, Tennessee. We both were working in the music business. Louise was managing the office for a recording and publishing company and I was singing with a gospel group. We had been talking for a while about starting our family. This is something we had discussed even before we got married. We both definitely wanted children. Several months went by with no success, so Louise's doctor referred us to the Vanderbilt University Medical Center. After months of testing, we were given the news, that in all probability, there would not be any children. It was devastating news to us, especially to Louise. She had so much wanted to be a mother. I couldn't begin to tell you the times I held her while she cried. I would tell her, "Honey, stop crying. God has a purpose for this, so we need to put it in His hands," and she agreed that's what we would do. It's easy looking back now and it sounds like I was brave and spiritual, but to tell you the truth, I was hurting too. It was hard not to ask God, "Why?"

Well, sixteen years went by and still no baby. We had resolved ourselves to the fact it would be just the two of us. However, God had another plan, and I love His plan. But guess what? God doesn't always reveal His plans to us. As a matter of fact, He seldom ever does. That's when the trust factor has to kick in. It's so amazing to sit back and watch as His plan unfolds right before our eyes, and that's what was just about to happen to us.

The month of our 22nd anniversary, Louise got a phone call one day from her sister, Annette, and she asked the question, "If you and Billy could get a newborn baby, would you be at all interested?" Louise asked her if she could call back

44

the next day because she needed to talk to me. I remember getting home from work that night and she said, "Honey, I got a phone call today and I need to ask you a question. If we could get a newborn baby, do you think we might be interested?" In a split second, without thinking about it, I said "yes". Then I asked a bunch of questions such as who, what, when, where, why and how? She proceeded to tell me about a young fourteen year old girl who found herself in an unexpected and unwanted pregnancy all because of a one-time mistake. The next day when Annette called back, Louise told her, "YES, we definitely want the baby." I didn't know if it was a boy or girl or if it was a healthy baby or not. It didn't make any difference at all. I think I fell in love with that baby immediately.

In a private adoption the birth mother has to meet the adoptive parents. A minister's wife was helping to make all the arrangements for the adoption so we met at her home. From the day they called to tell us what time to be there, Louise and I were both very nervous and anxious. We were afraid the young girl might not like us, or since I was 44 and Louise was 40, she might think we were too old and decide she didn't want us to have the baby. When we arrived she was already there with her mother. She looked like a little doll. My heart went out to her. She was so nervous and scared. We talked for a while and had the opportunity to ask questions. We tried to make her feel as comfortable as possible. When it was time to go we asked if we could have prayer with her. Louise and I stood with our arms around her and asked God to be with her and make everything go easy and give her peace. We also prayed for our baby. The best I remember, it was several days before we found out that she really liked us and wanted us to have the baby. We were told that the due date was the latter part of January.

I guess you know where we went next. Yep, you're right, looking at baby clothes, cribs and anything else pertaining to babies. Whenever we went grocery shopping before, we seldom went down the aisle with all the baby food and diapers because there was really no need to, but that all changed.

Since we lived in North Carolina we had to satisfy the laws of both states, Virginia and North Carolina. We had hired a lawyer to take care of everything, but Louise ended up doing most of the work. She was office manager for the legal department at Blue Cross Blue Shield of North Carolina in Chapel Hill. She pretty much knew what to do with help from lawyers in the legal department. You wouldn't believe some of the things that had to be done, such as contacting the Cherokee Indian Reservation in North Carolina and Oklahoma to see if there was any objection to the adoption since the baby was one-sixteenth Cherokee Indian. It was quite an ordeal, but Louise did a great job.

We couldn't wait for January. We were counting the days. We had all the legal requirements taken care of and everything was in order. Now it was a matter of waiting and waiting and waiting. They told us they would call as soon as she went into labor. January came and passed with no baby. All kinds of thoughts went through our heads. We wondered if she had changed her mind. I slept with the phone next to my pillow every night. Looking back now, I think Louise handled the waiting part better than I did. On Wednesday, February 5, 1992, we got home from work and as usual, I ran to the answering machine. There were about five messages. The last one said, "Get to Newport News, Virginia as fast as you can. She's at the hospital in labor." As you might guess we already had our bags packed and ready to go. I think that was the first time we ever made that trip without me being fussed at for speeding. Instead of hitting her invisible brakes, Louise was sitting over there pressing her invisible accelerator. We arrived at the hospital around 10:00 that night. The birth Mother's Dad would go in the birthing room, check on her, then come back and tell us how she was doing. It was around 11:00 when he came out and asked us to follow him. I asked, "Where are we going?" He said, "My daughter said this is going to be your baby and for me to bring you in. She wants you to be here for the birth." At 4:11 on Thursday morning, February 6, 1992 we watched our 7 lb. 6 oz. little girl come into the world. We already had a name picked out for a boy and one for a girl. We named her Angela Lynette Jones, after her birth mother, my sister Lynell, and Louise's sister, Annette.

I can tell you one thing with no hesitation and no reservation. We can trust God. When we place our cares in His hands, we can rest assured that He will do what is best for us. He loves us too much to do otherwise. He's never made a mistake. He's never been early, and He's never been late. He's always right-on-time.

If Satan had been allowed to carry out his plan, Angel would not be here today. Isn't it amazing how God can take what Satan meant for our harm and destruction and turn it into something beautiful and good? Why doesn't everybody want to serve Him?

There is so much more I could say, but let me end with this. God knows the end from the beginning. Nothing catches Him by surprise. What He wants for us is so much better, grander and sweeter than anything we could ever want for ourselves. If it delights us when God answers our prayers, how much more does it delight Him when we place our trust and faith in Him for the answer to our prayers? Glory to His precious and holy name!

I would like to take this opportunity to say thank you to Angel's birth mother. Words cannot begin to express our gratitude for what you have given to us. The privilege to be Mother and Father to the most wonderful daughter any man or woman could ever wish for is more than we could have ever dreamed of. I cannot imagine the past eighteen years without her in our lives. There's only been one other gift that's ever been given to us that's more precious than the gift you gave, and that's the gift of God's son, Jesus, our Lord and Savior. Again we say, Thank You!

**Angela Lynette Jones
Eighteen Years Old**

ANGEL'S SONG

by Billy C. Jones

(Recorded by Billy & Louise and

played at Angel's Dedication Service)

(I sang this verse)

For so long we dreamed of hearing the news

You're going to be Mommy and Dad,

But when we were told

There will be no child to hold

Our hearts were so heavy and sad.

More than anything in the world

We wanted a boy or girl

To have, to love, to hold

But if this can never be

Then Lord please help me

To accept what your will unfolds.

(Louise sang this verse)

And then one day

I heard somebody say

Would you like a little baby of your own?

A precious young girl

Will bring a child into the world

And she wants it to have a Christian home.

When they told her about us

She said I will entrust

My baby into their care

Now I know what is meant

By the words "Heaven sent"

Our little Angel surely came from there.

(chorus)

Thank you Lord

For our bundle of joy

She's Daddy's little girl

The sunshine in mommy's world

And so much more

With our friends and family

We bring Angel to Thee

Our hearts are so glad

That we're her Mom and Dad

So we can give her to Thee

And now we dedicate her to Thee.

A FISHING TRIP I WILL NEVER FORGET

From June of 1960 to June of 1963, my Dad pastored the North Henderson Pentecostal Holiness Church in Henderson, North Carolina. It was Saturday, May 11, 1963. I was 15 years old, my brother Byron was 14, and my baby brother Harold was 10. We, along with two other brothers, Butch and Mike Pridgen, were helping Gene Gupton, a neighbor, wash his car. Gene had a 1957 Chevy two door hardtop. Now you talk about a beautiful car, that car was beautiful. The fenders in front and back had been customized. It had thirteen coats of hand rubbed black paint with red and black roll pleated leather interior. It had a brand new 1963 Corvette motor in it. We worked all morning on that car and we had it looking good. Gene was 21 years old and took up a lot of time with the boys in our neighborhood. When we finished working on the car he told us to go ask our parents if we could go fishing. He told us what time to be back at his house with our fishing gear. This was our reward for helping him wash his car. I remember loading our fishing gear into the trunk. We were kidding around about who was going to catch the biggest fish. Gene loved to go fishing but he was scared to death to touch one. If he caught a fish we would have to take it off the hook for him. There's another story I'll have to tell you about Gene and me going frog gigging, but I'll save that until later.

We were a little bit late leaving, but we finally got on the road around 4:00 that afternoon. I was sitting in the front seat on the passenger's side, Butch was sitting in the middle, and Gene was driving. Byron was sitting in the back seat behind Gene, Harold was in the middle, and Mike was sitting right behind me. We were riding along having a good time and listening to the radio. I remember Neil Sedaka was singing, *Let's Go Steady Again*, on the radio. All of a sudden we saw a car coming around the curve at a high rate of speed. He ran off the road on his side and started back across the road coming straight for us. Gene had run off on the right side of the highway trying to miss him, but it was too late. He hit us head on. When I regained consciousness, the motor was under my feet and the car was smoking really bad. I couldn't see or hear very well because blood was in my eyes and my ears. Someone came to my window and said get out quick, the car is going to catch on fire. The doors were jammed shut so we had to climb out the windows. Byron was trying to get out on the driver's side, but Gene kept saying, "No, get out on the other side." Gene was a fireman for the city and was trying to help put the fire out. I think he was in shock and thought he was at work. They had to make him lay down until they could put him in the ambulance. I remember laying there on the ground and Harold was on his knees looking down at me. The jolt from the impact had caused him to bite his tongue, and blood was running out of his mouth. He kept trying to say something to me, but I had trouble understanding him. I finally understood him to say, "You are bleeding really bad, but don't worry you're going to be all right". He was crying because he was scared and hurting, and I was scared because every time my heart would beat, blood would shoot out the side of my head. Harold stuck right there with me though.

Later on we found out why Gene didn't want anybody getting out on the driver's side. The man who was driving the other vehicle was lying beside our car dead. There were two passengers in the other car and both of them were so drunk they could hardly walk. There were two couples who tried to stop them from leaving the lake, but they couldn't, so they followed them to see how far they would get.

Mom and Dad were standing out in the yard with our two year old little sister, Lynell. All of a sudden, four ambulances, several police cars, and fire trucks went by our house. Daddy said, "There must be a bad wreck somewhere". Mom said, "You don't reckon it could be the boys, do you?" Daddy said, "No, they've had plenty of time to get to the lake." He didn't know we were late leaving. A short time later Gene's wife came running into the yard screaming, "Gene's had a wreck! Gene's had a wreck!" Not long after that, the first ambulance came by headed to the hospital. That's the one I was in. Our neighbors ran over and got Lynell so Mom and Dad could go to the hospital. It was about that time the other ambulances came by. On the way to the hospital, mom turned the radio on and they announced there had been a bad wreck on Satterwhite Point Road with one known dead and a number injured. Mom and Dad knew they had three boys in the wreck. When Mom and Dad got to the hospital the stop light in front of the emergency room was red. About that time Daddy saw them push somebody back into one of the ambulances and shut the door. He jumped out of the car, ran across the street and asked the driver who it was.

He said, "I'm sorry, but I don't know his name." Back then they didn't have ambulances like we have today. They were hearses, with a red light on top, operated by funeral homes. There was no such thing as a rescue squad.

After Daddy parked the car, he and Mom ran to the emergency room. They saw Byron and Harold in the hallway waiting to be taken in. They ran straight to them to see how bad they were hurt. They had cuts all over their faces from flying glass. Then Dad asked where I was. He told me later that was the hardest question to ask because he just knew that it was me they rolled back into the ambulance. When Byron told him where I was, he asked the nurse to take him to me. I was so glad to see him, but not nearly as glad as he was to see me. Later on that night he said, "Boy, you were a bloody mess, but I've never been so glad to see you."

While I was lying on the side of the road thinking that I was going to bleed to death, something came to my mind that my Daddy told the three of us boys just a week or so before. We had gotten to the place where we fussed and fought all the time. We couldn't get along with each other at all. Daddy told us that if we didn't start loving one another and being kind to one another something bad was going to happen.

Now, I'm not going to sit here and tell you that we never had another disagreement, but that wreck drove that message home. I shiver to think that I could have lived the rest of my life without Byron or Harold, or that I could have died that day. I try to call them every two or three days and I always tell them I love them when we talk, and I give them a big old bear hug when I see them. You never know when it could be your last chance to tell someone that you love them. Don't ever let that opportunity pass you by. You may regret it the rest of your life.

**This is the car we were in. Byron is
telling mom something about the wreck.**

THE ONE AND ONLY TIME I EVER WENT FROG GIGGING

৩৻৩

Late one night Gene Gupton and I decided to go frog gigging. Gene knew where a pond was, but it was posted with no trespassing signs, so we had to sneak in from the back side of the farm. I carried the flashlight and the bucket to put the frogs in. I was going to spot the frogs for Gene. Instead of a frog gig, Gene was going to shoot them with his rifle. We were trying to be real quiet as we walked along the bank looking for frogs. I think we forgot about one important thing. The sound of the rifle was going to alert someone that we were there. All of a sudden, we looked up and there was a man coming towards us with a flashlight in one hand and a shotgun in the other. It was too late for us to run, so we just stood there. To tell you the truth I was so scared I don't think I could have run. As he approached us, he kept stumbling like he was about to fall down, and when he got to us, we realized he was drunk. Not only did he have a problem walking, but he also had a problem talking. We could hardly understand a thing he was saying. He wanted to know what we were doing there, so Gene told him who we were and that we were frog gigging. He said, "That's no problem I'll help you. Come on and follow me." This man's job was to keep an eye on the place and keep trespassers out. He was really doing a good job. He took us around to a row boat and told us to get in. He said he would row along the bank and we could shoot the frogs from the boat. Why in the world we got in that boat with a drunk I will never know. I was very nervous. No, I was plumb scared to death, because neither Gene nor I could swim, and our new friend was so drunk he couldn't swim. He also had a problem keeping the boat close to the bank where the frogs would be. He couldn't row the boat any straighter than he could walk.

Now, this is where it really got bad. I don't know if you realize it or not, but a flashlight shining on the water at night will draw fish to the light. This was not good because Gene was scared of a fish. Because of the weight of three people in that little boat, it was sitting very low in the water. All of a sudden fish started jumping out of the water towards the light, and yep you guessed it, one landed in the boat.

Now folks, when you've got a drunk paddling the boat, and a man with a rifle trying to get away from a fish that's flopping around in the bottom of the boat, you've got a recipe for disaster. I'm sure we looked like Otis, Barney and Andy. I was trying to catch that little fish so I could throw it back in the water before Gene turned the boat over or started shooting at it.

Well, obviously we made it back to the shore. We bid our drunk friend good bye and headed for home. I don't know if it was my imagination or what, but it sure sounded like those frogs were laughing at us as we walked away. They all lived to see another day, and I've never been frog gigging since then and don't ask me to go. I learned a lesson. When a sign says "NO TRESPASSING", stay out!

A COKE BOTTLE,
FISHING LINE AND SPAM

❧❧

I've always enjoyed fishing, and although I've never considered myself really good at it, I've always wanted to learn more. According to the fishing shows I've watched on T.V. there are certain things that are a must if you are going to be a fisherman. There are certain rods and reels that you've got to have if you are going to catch certain kinds of fish. I guess each species knows which line is meant for them and which line is off limits. You must have a heavy rod and reel with heavy line to bring in those big catfish, and light gear is a must for catching pan fish. I learned this from watching, "Bill Dance Outdoors." But when it comes to catching bass, now that's a whole different story. You've got to match the bait or lures to the fishing conditions, such as the weather and the water temperature. Are you impressed yet? Again, you must have the correct rod and reel for certain bait. To be properly prepared, you really need about fifteen different rods and reels, ready at all times, with an assortment of about five hundred types of artificial bait of different sizes, shapes, colors and flavors.

Now we can forget about one of those 500hp bass boats. There's no way I could afford one of those anyway. Speaking of boats, there is one question I wish somebody would answer for me. Why is it that people fishing from the bank try to see how far they can throw their line out into the lake, and people out in a boat try to see how close to the bank they can throw theirs? I've never understood that.

Up to this point, I've shared with you some truth, mixed with a little bit of sarcasm. OK, a whole lot of sarcasm, but I'd like to tell you about an event that took place about twenty years ago that taught me more than all those fishing shows on T.V. I had purchased one of those hundred dollar rod and reels and a tackle box full of the latest gadgets and gismos that are guaranteed to catch more and bigger fish. There was a large pond behind our house that I enjoyed going to, just to practice my techniques for overhand casting, underhand casting, flipping, and a number of other techniques and maneuvers that you nonprofessionals would not understand. Have I mentioned I never missed an episode of "Bill Dance

Outdoors?" I was becoming a professional fisherman so fast it was almost scary.

One afternoon I was at the pond practicing when I heard footsteps coming up from behind me. When I turned around, there stood a Mexican gentleman who lived not far from us. He was carrying a five gallon bucket in his hand. I wasn't sure if he was planning to dip the fish out of the pond or what, but I thought I would take this opportunity to show off my new equipment and my new found skills in the art of fishing. I made three or four casts way out into the pond and retrieved each one with a jerking motion to imitate a wounded fish. Bill Dance would have been so proud. About that time, my new fishing buddy reached into his bucket and pulled out a coke bottle with fishing line wrapped around it. I thought to myself, "What in the world is this dummy fixin' to do?" He had a hook and a great big chunk of lead on the end of the line and about two feet from that he had a red and white bobber. I'm not sure what that stuff was he was using for bait, but it looked like dried up spam. What he did next was unbelievable. With his left hand he held the coke bottle up in the air, slightly tilted towards the pond, and with his right hand he started whirling that chunk of lead and dried spam over his head like a helicopter. Once he got it up to full speed it kinda sounded like a helicopter. I didn't know if he was going to fly that thing or if he was trying to lasso fish. When he finally let go, it went way out into the pond, about as far as my hundred dollar rod and reel. He let it sit there for a minute and then started wrapping the line around that coke bottle as he reeled it in with a jerking motion. All of a sudden, that red and white bobber went out of sight and he reeled in a nice frying size fish. I don't remember exactly how many times that happened, but he ended up with enough fish for his family to have a good meal. Well, as for me, I didn't get a single bite. As he walked away, I felt like asking him if he wanted to trade fishing gear, but decided I could probably make my own.

I've thought about the events of that afternoon quite a bit. What was the difference? Why did he catch fish and I didn't? Oh, I know there are all kinds of answers we could give, and there would probably be some truth and logic in all of them, but I think it all boils down to one thing and that's the "WHY". Why was I there? And why was my Mexican friend there? What was the motivating factor for either one of us? For me it was for fun and sport, nothing big or important, just having a good time. But for my new friend, it was much more than that, it was his family. Putting food on the table for his wife and two kids is not only what motivated him, but it inspired him. You see, motivation comes from an outward stimulus, but to be inspired, now that comes from within. His family was his "WHY". His wife and children are what inspired him.

I've heard my good friend, Ken Raynor, say on so many occasions over the past twenty years, the thing that kept him going when he wanted to throw his hands up and quit working his business was a picture of his two little girls, Mary and Kenzie, that he had taped to the steering wheel of his car. He said, "Every time I got tired, discouraged and felt like I could not drive another mile or do another meeting, I looked down and saw their little faces and it reignited that fire within me, and I was ready to go do it all over again." I believe that most, if not all of our failures in life, are a direct result of failing to identify our "WHY". It wasn't our lack of skills. We only become skillful at something by doing it over and over and over. No one is skillful at anything when they first start. The real problem is, we never sat down and identified our "WHY." What is it that puts that fire in your belly? That makes you unstoppable? My Mexican friend said, "I can't afford a hundred dollars for fishing equipment, so I'll have to make do with what I have available. All I know is someway, somehow my family will have fish for supper tonight." You know what? I bet those fish were delicious!

You may not be a great orator with great eloquence of speech, and you may not possess a great vocabulary. That's OK! Just identify your "WHY" and then take what you do have, even if it's just a coke bottle, fishing line, and dried spam and go conquer your world.

In loving memory
Kenneth McDonald Raynor ~ Friend & Mentor
November 4, 1950 – April 13, 2010

David Alan Jones

MY SPECIAL BROTHER

T he morning of July 5, 1968 sticks out in my mind so vividly. I was standing in formation with E Company, 1st Battalion, 1st Brigade, at Fort Bragg, North Carolina. I was in my second week of basic training. All of a sudden I heard a Drill Sergeant scream out my name. Whenever a Drill Sergeant screams out your name, in most cases, it is not a good thing. Usually, it means you are in big trouble. I replied in the meanest, deepest, military voice I could muster up. "Right here Drill Sergeant." I probably sounded more like Gomer Pyle. He began to read from a piece of paper, "Private Jones, you have a new baby brother born this morning. Mother and brother are doing fine." I was very shocked, because it was too soon. The due date was still a month and a half away. Oh, by the way, I still have that note he read from. I couldn't wait to call Dad and get all the details.

Well, two weeks later Mom, Dad, my little sister Lynell, and my brother Harold brought David Alan Jones to see me. I'll never forget when Mom handed him to me the first time. I was very, very nervous because he was so tiny. He weighed a little less than 5lbs. when he was born. He was so little he looked like a little baby doll.

David and Me at Ft. Bragg, N.C.

I don't know how my Mom did all she had to do. She had a seven year old daughter to take care of, a son in high school, a son in Bible College, and me in the Army. She prayed for each one of us every day, and she felt like she just had to write to Byron and me every day. Along with all of this and teaching a Sunday School class, she now had a newborn baby to take care of.

When David was about a year and a half old, his behavior began to change. He stopped doing the things babies his age would normally be doing. He stopped talking and he would sit and rock back and forth all the time. He made no eye contact at all and there was no exchange of affection. As he got older, he wanted everything to remain the same, no changes at all. His behavior continued to get worse. Sometimes he would cry for hours and hours without stopping. My Dad was pastoring the Gretna Pentecostal Holiness Church in Gretna, Virginia at this particular time. The people were so kind and understanding. They helped Mom every way they could.

Well, time marched on and my Dad was sent to pastor the Mt. Calvary Pentecostal Holiness Church in Axton, Virginia. It took David quite a while to get over moving. The older David got, the more difficult he became to handle. To quote my Mom, "When he was good he was good, but when he was bad he was terrible." I've seen my mother sit and cry uncontrollably because she didn't think she could take anymore. She would start praying and before long she would be OK.

If it had not been for Lynell, Mom and Dad would have had to put David in a home for the mentally handicapped. She was always there when they needed her. She never dated or went out. You might say she put her life on hold to help take care of David. But you know what? I've never once heard her complain, not once. There was a special bond between her and her little brother that remains intact to this day. Raising a special needs child is a full-time job. It leaves little, if no time at all, for anything else.

The doctors finally sent David to the University of Virginia to be evaluated. I'll never forget Mom crying all the way home, because a doctor there told her David's biggest problem was, he was a spoiled brat. She knew something was wrong, but nobody knew what it was. Finally, he was sent to the University of North Carolina at Chapel Hill and after weeks of testing, it was found that he was Autistic. Mom and Dad had never heard of Autism, but tried to learn all they could about this mental disorder. It wasn't as prevalent then as it is today. I remember someone once asked my mother what was wrong with David, and when she told them he was Autistic, they replied, "Oh, my little boy loves to draw too."

I couldn't begin to tell you all the things David did. Some were embarrassing, but you quickly learned to get over that. Some of the things he did were funny, such as the time Mom and Dad took him to Shoney's to eat. Mom was following the hostess to their table and David was walking behind Mom. Daddy had stopped to speak to someone he knew. When he looked up, David had stopped at a man's table, picked up his glass of tea, and drank the whole thing. When he finished, he set the glass down and went on to their table. Dad rushed to the gentleman's table and began to apologize. He was very nice and understanding, which cannot be said about everyone they encountered.

On another occasion, all the family went down to Greensboro, N.C. to meet my brother Byron and his wife Marinas at a restaurant. The hostess seated us at a large table right in the middle of the dining room. Sometime during the course of the meal, David informed not only us, but everyone else close by, that he needed to go to the restroom. I was elected to go with him. If I get too graphic, I apologize, but I've got to tell you this. There was only one stall in the men's room. David went in and got all situated, and I stood in front of the stall with the door opened so I could see him in case he needed help. Even though David was in his mid twenties at that time, we all still called him sugar, honey, baby, sweetie, or some endearing name, and as a matter of fact, we still do. Even though he's 41 years old now, he's still our baby. David had been seated there for quite a while, and I was ready to get back to my meal. In the meantime, a man had come in the restroom and was occupied at the other relief station. You know, the one where you stand at. From where I was, I could see David and I could also see the gentleman who had joined us. Without thinking how it might sound or look, I said to David, "Honey, are you finished yet? Hurry up baby, we've got to go." I think our friend froze right where he was. I saw him slowly turn his head towards the stall and look down at the floor. Since the stall didn't go all the way to the floor, he could see David's size eleven shoes. I don't think he finished what he had come in there for. He quickly put everything away and went out the door as fast as he could. He didn't even stop to wash his hands. I could feel eyes staring at us as we made our way back to our table.

I felt a need to share that with you. Using the word "share" gives it a religious connotation, which that story definitely needed.

In 1982, Daddy was sent to pastor the Swansonville Pentecostal Holiness Church. This was quite an adjustment for David. Any kind of a change really upset him. It took months and sometimes even a year for him to fully adjust to changes. The people at the church were so kind and understanding. By this time, David was a teenager and had gotten quite tall. He and Mom had their own pew they sat on, or should I say Mom sat on. David stretched out with his head in Mom's lap.

In July of 1984, Mom's health began to fail. She was suffering with congestive heart failure and she was diabetic. On Friday, Sept. 7th, she came home after a twenty-nine day stay in the hospital. David was so happy to see his mother. We couldn't take him to the hospital to see Mom because he would get upset in a strange place, and he would want her to come home. Mom was so happy to see David. There was a special love between those two like I've never seen before.

On Saturday afternoon, Esther Nichols, from the Mt. Calvary Pentecostal Holiness Church, came to fix Mom's hair. Mom asked Lynell if she would fix something to eat before doing her hair because she felt so weak. David would come in the dining room to see Mom, then go back to his room, and then come back to check on her again. He did this over and over. Each time he would have to touch her, then laugh and clap his hands. He was so glad to have her home.

While Mom was eating, Lynell asked her how her meal tasted and she replied, "It's delicious! Thank you so much!"

Then all of a sudden, she started falling over. Lynell called for Daddy who ran in from the kitchen just in time to catch her in his arms. He laid her on the floor and made several attempts to revive her, but she was gone. Keeping David out of the room was difficult. Mom was lying on the floor and he didn't understand why.

Mom's funeral was planned for Monday, September 10, 1984. Daddy and Lynell decided it was best not to take David to the funeral, but Daddy wanted us to take him to the funeral home to see Mom. On Sunday morning, Lynell went to Sunday School. She said that's what Mom would have wanted, because up to that time, she had perfect attendance and Mom wouldn't want her to miss. When she came home, Lynell, Harold and I took David to the funeral home. On the way there we tried to prepare him, but he did not understand. All he knew was he was going to see Mama. When we walked into the funeral home and David saw his mother, he ran to her casket and got her by the hand and said, "Go home Mama." There was not a dry eye in that place. Even the men who worked for the funeral home were crying. He knew something was wrong because she felt cold and she didn't move. David stood at Mom's casket for a good while. He would reach over and touch her face and whisper to her.

After a while, we told him to sit down with us. Finally, when it was time to leave, we told David to tell Mama good bye. I could tell he was getting upset when he said in a loud voice, "Mama, go home." Lynell said, "Mama's gone to see Jesus. She can't go home." David looked at her and said, "David go see Jesus. Mama, go home." Finally he reached down and kissed her and said "Goodbye Mama." Then he walked out.

It took David a year or longer to adjust. He stood by the front door and waited for Mom to come home. Every time he heard a car, he would say "Mama's home."

I know taking care of David was very hard on Mom, and I believe she would have lived a lot longer if not for the strain of caring for David, but she wouldn't have had it any other way. She was only 56 years old when she died. She's been gone twenty-six years now, but David still remembers and misses her.

On August 22, 2000 we suffered another devastating loss. At about 2:20 that afternoon, we stood by Daddy's hospital bed and watched him take that journey I've heard him preach about all my life.

We took David to the funeral home to see Dad, but not to the funeral. The concept of death did not register with David at all. He took Dad's death better than mother's because at that time he was living in a group home in Danville, Virginia, and was used to being away from Dad and the family, although he did come home every weekend or so.

David is 42 years old now and continues to live in a group home in Danville, Virginia. Lynell picks him up once a month for a weekend visit, but he's always ready to go back to his home.

I thank God for my brothers and sister. I call them almost every day because I don't want to ever lose that closeness we've always had. I'm so proud of each one of them. Byron and his wife, Marinas, have been married 38 years and live in Fairview, North Carolina where Byron pastors Truth Worship Center. They have a beautiful home on the side of a mountain close to their daughter Anna, her husband Jimmy, and their son Dakota.

Harold and his wife, Margie, have been married 37 years and live in Forest, Virginia. They have such a beautiful home. Their daughter and son-in-law, Shawn and Joe Horrell, are the pastors at their church. They have three precious children, Tony, Jason, and Kaley. Harold and Margie's son, Doug, his wife Dee, and their daughter, Alexis, also attend their church. What a blessing to be able to worship with your children and grandchildren every Sunday.

Lynell and her husband, Mark, have been married six years and live in Buffalo Ridge, Virginia. They attend the Buffalo Ridge Pentecostal Holiness Church. Lynell teaches special education at Patrick County High School. She and Mark have a beautiful home and are so happy.

Louise, Angel, and I live in Dry Fork, Virginia where we attend the Swansonville Pentecostal Holiness Church. We are enjoying the blessings of God.

I guess the thing I am most thankful for, is the fact that all of my family are saved and serving the Lord.

Sometimes, I wonder what it would have been like if David had been normal with a family of his own, but then I have to remember, God has a purpose for everything and everybody. This is the purpose God chose for David. I don't understand it, and maybe we're not supposed to understand it. As Mom would so emphatically say, "You don't question God! He knows what He is doing."

I'm just as proud of David and his accomplishments as I am the rest of the family. He's done the best he could do with what he has been given, and folks, when you've done the best you can do, you can't do any better than that.

A LESSON I HAD TO
LEARN THE HARD WAY

I have a dear friend, just a little older than I am, who once told me she got saved when she was four years old, and that she's been serving the Lord ever since. She also said, "I can't think of one thing in my life I would change even if I were given the opportunity to go back and do so." I've thought to myself so many times, "Oh, how I wish I could say that." There have been so many decisions that I've made and things I've done in my past that I have to admit, I never prayed about. I just did it. If it was what I wanted or what I wanted to do then I went for it full speed ahead. Looking back now I find myself thinking, "Oh, how I wish I could go back and change the past." I would do some things so differently, but I can't. I feel as though I've run in circles and gotten nowhere. But maybe by writing down my innermost thoughts and feelings, and yes even my regrets, I can help someone else realize the importance of seeking God and His will. I really believe I was afraid to seek God's will in some matters, because I was afraid He would say "No", when I wanted Him to say "Yes", and I was afraid He would say "Yes", when I wanted Him to say "No". I learned the hard way that we must always pray until we have clear direction from God concerning His will for our lives. If we don't, we can find ourselves in serious trouble, and as a result, we will waste a lot of what could have been productive years.

One such decision was when I moved to Nashville, Tennessee. Before we got married, I told Louise that when I got out of the Army, my dream was to be a full-time gospel singer. I never prayed about it. From the time I was a little boy, that's all I've ever wanted to do. I don't know why, but I've always had this idea that God won't call you to do anything that you love to do. There's no sacrifice in that.

Everybody knows if you are going to be a singer, you've got to be in Nashville, at least that's what I thought. When I told Louise that I was ready to make the move, she said, "If that's what you really want, then we'll go." She's never told me this, but looking back, I don't think she really wanted us to go. When I told my Dad what I was going to do, he said, "Son, I think you are making a big mistake. You don't belong out there. I really don't think you should go." Well, that sealed the deal. I was going no matter what. I look back now and it's so clear to me that my attitude was so wrong, but I couldn't see it then. I knew what I wanted to do, and nobody was going to stop me. Some people may think that's an admirable quality, but not necessarily so. I flew to Nashville and rented an apartment. We sold our house, loaded our furniture into a U-haul truck and off we went. I was going to prove to my Daddy that he was wrong.

Well, I was able to do what I dreamed of doing. I was with several groups, but it wasn't like I thought it would be at all. On one tour when I was with a trio, we sang every night with the exception of one for six straight weeks. The one night we were off we went to hear another group in Detroit, Michigan. We came home for a few days and then we left for three weeks. Our last weekend out, Louise flew to Kansas City and we picked her up at the airport after our Friday night concert. I was so glad to see her. She was with us for Saturday and Sunday and then we came home.

I hated leaving Louise by herself while I was out on the road. Finally, I just quit the group. I told them I was never leaving my wife for months at a time again. The next group I was with it was a little bit better. I was actually their road manager. Most of the time we would leave Nashville on Wednesday afternoon or Wednesday night, depending on how far we had to travel for Thursday night's concert. Thursday, Friday, and Saturday night concerts were usually in coliseums or school auditoriums, and were booked by our booking agency who kept us very busy. At one time we had eight songs from our latest album in the top ten on the gospel charts. The other two songs were a little further down. According to the major charts and radio play from all over the country, plus our record sales, we were ranked the number one Southern Gospel group in the country at that time. Our booking agency capitalized on that because they got a percentage of our fee for the dates they booked for us. The busier they kept us, the more the agency made, and believe me they kept us booked up. A lot of our dates were so far apart we had to drive all night and all day as fast as we could go just to get there in time to set up our sound equipment and product tables. We had a full-time bus driver so we could sleep while traveling. My bunk was right over the engine in the back of the bus. As long as it was running, I slept like a baby, but if it stopped, I'd wake up. When we were at home, sleeping was sometimes a problem. I almost needed someone to shake the bed and hum real loud so I could sleep. It was nothing to go to bed in Dallas and get up in Atlanta, Georgia. I remember one time we ended a west coast tour in Vancouver, British Columbia in Canada, and we had three and a half days to get to Birmingham, Alabama. The only time we stopped was to fuel the bus up. When our bus driver got tired, he would slide out from behind the wheel, and one of us would slide in and never slow down. We had to get enough food at each truck stop to last until our next stop for fuel. Thank goodness we only did a west coast tour once each year.

Most of the time we would book a church for Sunday night on our way back home. On Sunday morning, we were traveling from our Saturday night concert to our Sunday night singing, so we couldn't go to church. If we were in church, it was to sing, and not to be ministered to. Our spiritual welfare was not the booking agency's main concern. They were in business to make money.

It wouldn't be an exaggeration if I said I went as much as a year and didn't hear one sermon. I died spiritually because I was not being fed. I would not have admitted this at that time, but I was in a backslidden condition, and I was calling myself out working for the Lord.

It makes no difference if you are a singer, evangelist or involved in some other type of full time ministry. You must set aside time to feed the spiritual man, or what some refer to as the inner man. Even Pastors need to take time off to be ministered to. Nobody gives more of themselves on a daily basis than Pastors. There's always somebody who needs or wants their time and attention, day and night, but we all know that's a part of being a Pastor, don't we? I remember when I was a young boy, our family was about to leave going on vacation and someone in the church got sick or died, and my Dad had to cancel our vacation. My little brother, Harold, said, "Every time we plan something, somebody gets sick, dies, or wants to get married." He was about right, although we knew it couldn't be helped.

Trying to be all things to all people is spiritually and physically draining. That's why you have to take a break ever so often. In other words, as my Dad would say, "You've got to get your batteries recharged." You can't do this on your own with books and tapes either. You cannot give and give and give, because you will eventually give out. When you do the same routine night, after night, after night, if you're not careful, it becomes just that, a routine and you will find yourself faking it. The songs you sing, or sermons you preach must have a fresh anointing and the only way that will happen is to be fed on God's word and sit under Holy Ghost anointed preaching on a regular basis. Just as the physical man needs to be nourished, so does the spiritual man.

Please listen very carefully right here. This is so important. For anything that has beauty, value, or that is considered precious, there will be a counterfeit or an imitation for it. This you can count on. For example, a beautiful red rose requires care and attention. It has to be watered, nurtured and pruned or trimmed to grow and retain its beauty. It gives off a sweet fragrance because it is alive. It is the real thing! But then there's the counterfeit. It requires no watering, nurturing, or care of any kind. It does not grow or give off that sweet aroma because it is not real. Oh, it looks like the real thing, from a distance, but upon closer examination the truth is revealed; it's just a red silk rose, an imitation. I'm afraid there are a lot of imitations out there calling themselves working for the Lord.

Nothing sparkles like a diamond, but one must be very careful. There is an imitation or counterfeit for this precious stone, and the difference cannot be detected from a distance. It takes close examination by a trained eye or you could be deceived. Then, there's currency or money. It's of value, and enough of it can buy most anything you desire, but beware, there is such a thing as counterfeit money, and unless you know what to look for, you could be deceived into thinking it is real.

Let me ask you a silly question. Have you ever seen counterfeit or imitation trash or garbage? You are probably thinking, "That is a silly question. Of course not, because there's no beauty or value and there's surely nothing precious about it." You are exactly right. Here's my point. The things of God are of great beauty, they are of great value, and they are most precious. Because of this truth, I can assure you that Satan has a counterfeit or an imitation for the beautiful, valuable, and precious things of God. Satan wants to sell us an imitation for what is real, and many people are being deceived and are not even aware of it. Before we accept anything and everything that comes along, we need to do some close examination through the eyes of God's word to be sure it is of God. If it is of God, He will put His stamp of approval on it. His stamp of approval is called, "The Anointing."

Knowing God's will for our lives is of utmost importance. Sometimes it's not easy, but there is one sure way we can know. The more we seek the face of God and the closer we draw to Him, the easier it is to hear His voice and know His will. When we totally submit ourselves to Him and stay in His word, pray and seek His will, then we will recognize the genuine from the counterfeit that Satan has sold to so many.

WEDNESDAY NIGHT
PRAYER MEETING

I remember one summer back when I was a boy
I went to grandma's house to stay
And every morning after we ate breakfast
All the kids ran out to play
But there's one memory that means more to me
Than anybody knows,
It's the morning grandma asked me
If I'd help her hang out clothes

Her clothes line was tied to the woodshed
She gave the other end to me
And said, drag it across the backyard
And tie it to that tree,
And if you only remember one thing
You've ever learned from me

What I'm about to tell you
Is what I want it to be

You see, that old tree is Sunday
And the woodshed is Sunday too
And six long days are in between the two
And if it wasn't for one of the dearest friends
I have ever found
The clothes that hang in the middle
Would be dragging on the ground

Grandma handed me a long old stick
And said, "Here's my friend I was talking about
His name is Wednesday Night Prayer Meeting,"
And then she started to shout.
She said Wednesday night prayer meeting
Will lift you up above the ground
Up above the cares of life
When they try to pull you down
One thing I learned from my grandma
Is where new strength can be found
You can find it at prayer meeting
When Wednesday comes around

Well, Grandma's been gone for years now

And her old house is falling down

I went back just the other day

To reminisce and look around

Out behind the woodshed

You won't believe what I found

Wednesday Night Prayer Meeting

Laid rotting on the ground.

Then suddenly I heard a voice

As sad as it could be

It said, many modern day churches

Have done the same thing to me

Wednesday Night Prayer Meeting

Will lift you up above the ground

Up above the cares of life

When they try to pull you down

One thing I learned from my Grandma

Is where new strength can be found

You can find it at prayer meeting

When Wednesday comes around

So be sure you're at prayer meeting

When Wednesday night comes around

THE SADDEST BUT HAPPIEST DAY OF MY LIFE

After Louise and I moved from Nashville back to Danville, Virginia, I stayed in touch with one of my buddies who played in the band for one of the groups I was with. I don't remember if I called him, or if he called me on this particular occasion, but we had not talked in a while. He informed me that he was no longer in gospel music. He said he was playing guitar and singing backup for country singer, T. G. Sheppard, and writing country music. He said, "Now that's where the money is." When you write country songs you can write about anything, your dog, your pick-up truck, drinking, cheating or whatever. Nothing is off limits. He said, "You ought to give it a try." Well, that conversation planted a seed in my mind. (You have to admit, Satan is good at what he does. He always has someone to help push you in the wrong direction.) I'm not trying to put the blame on someone else. I'm the one who made the wrong choices.

Louise and I had started going to the Westover Hills Pentecostal Holiness Church in Danville, Virginia where my brother, Byron, was pastor. He asked me if I would be their choir director. I told him I would. Things seemed to be going pretty good, that is until I had that conversation with my buddy in Nashville. Every time we talked, he would tell me what country artist had recorded his songs. He told me that he was starting to make some very good money. Once when T.G. and Conway Twitty were in Greensboro at the coliseum, he got me free passes to hang out with him. I have to admit I was very impressed with the lights, glamour and the screaming crowd, and I wanted to be a part of that. I started getting very serious about writing country music. I knew if I was going to pursue this I would have to stop leading the choir, and the easiest way to do that was just quit going to church. I remember the Sunday I made my decision not to go back again. It was time to get ready to go to church and Louise was getting dressed. She said, "Honey, it's almost time to leave." I told her to go on by herself, that I wasn't going. She asked, "What's wrong? Are you sick?" I said, "No, I'm not sick. I'm just not going back anymore."

She started crying and wanted to know what was wrong. She asked, "Did I say something or do something to make you mad?" I told her, "No, I'm just not going back anymore."

Now I had another problem to deal with. I knew when Louise came home from church Byron and Marinas would be right behind her, and sure enough, I was right. I don't remember where I went, but I left the house and stayed gone until they were gone. I didn't want to face anybody or talk to anybody, but I knew sooner or later I had to face Mom and Dad. I dreaded that. I couldn't stand to see my Mom or Louise cry, especially when I was the cause.

Well, several years went by. Byron and Marinas had moved to Altavista, Virginia to pastor the Broad Street Pentecostal Holiness Church, and Mom and Dad had moved to the Swansonville Pentecostal Holiness Church. I was working in construction and trying to pursue my country music career. I had started going out to clubs on Friday and Saturday nights to get familiar with that kind of surroundings. How and why Louise put up with me during this time is a mystery to me. I was not a very good person. I guess there is one good thing I can say for myself. Although I was around drinking, I never did partake. To this day, I can honestly say

I've never had a swallow of alcohol in my life. I learned one thing for sure. My wife really and truly loves me.

I took what little money we had and what I could borrow, went back to Nashville and recorded a couple of records. My buddy was my producer and I used T.G.'s band. I justified spending all our money by telling myself it would make a good story about how I made it to the top.

Following are the lyrics to a couple of the country songs I wrote and recorded.

I REMEMBER YOUR SMILE

Verse one:

I remember your smile, it lit up your face

When I asked if you would wear my high school ring

I remember your smile, when I asked you to marry me

You didn't have to say a thing

I remember your smile

As you walked down the aisle

How lucky could one man ever be?

I looked at you and then said, "I do"

You squeezed my hand and smiled at me.

Verse two:

I remember your smile, the day you told me

We would bring a little one into the world

I remember your smile, when they said "It's a boy"

But you really wanted a girl

I remember your smile, when our little child

First walked without holding to your hand

Lord, what I'd give if I could just see

You smile like that once again.

Chorus:

I'm so hungry for your smile

It's been a while

And Lord it's really hurting me

It's been much too long

Something's gone wrong

I don't know what it could be

I've searched my mind trying to find

The words that I should say

I wish I knew what happened to you

And what took your smile away

Bridge:

I finally saw that beautiful smile

I've been wanting to see

I broke down and cried it hurts deep inside

'Cause you weren't smiling at me

Chorus:

I'm so hungry for your smile

It's been a while

And Lord it's really hurting me

It's been much too long

Something's gone wrong

I don't know what it could be

I've searched my mind

Trying to find

The words that I should say

I wish I knew what happened to you

And what took your smile away

DOES ANYBODY CARE?

I was sitting by my hotel window

Looking out on the people below

I saw a skinny old man with a cane in his hand

Dragging his feet so slow

He tipped his hat and said "Hi"

As the people pushed by

Then he stopped to catch his breath

I could tell he was poor

By the clothes that he wore

And then I thought to myself

Does anybody care?

Does anybody know his name?

Where does he stay?

Has he eaten today?

People it's a crying shame

Does anybody care

If his life is ending this way?

It's all up to you, now what'cha gonna do?

Does anybody care?

I ran down the stairs

Straight for the door

Into the busy street

With money in my hand

To give that old man

So he could get him something to eat

I searched high and low

Where did he go?

I lost him in the crowd

And there I stood

In the middle of the street

All the people heard me crying out loud.

Does anybody care?

Does anybody know his name?

Where does he stay?

Has he eaten today?

People it's a crying shame

Does anybody care

If his life is ending this way?

It's all up to you, now what'cha gonna do?

Does anybody care?

My work was all done

My flight left at one

I never saw him again

I didn't want to go

Why I don't know

It felt like I was leaving a friend

As my plane circled over the city

Taking me back home

The thought comes to mind

There's millions of his kind

Out there dying alone

Does anybody care?

Does anybody know his name?

Where does he stay?

Has he eaten today?

People it's a crying shame

Does anybody care

If his life is ending this way?

It's all up to you, now what'cha gonna do?

Does anybody care?

Well, I began to get some local radio play, but that's about all. I did have one song used on a national TV show on the Nashville Network, but that's the only success I ever had. I knew my Mom and Dad were praying for me, and because of that, I knew I didn't have a chance. The only real success I had in my life up to that point was my marriage, and I was putting that in danger and didn't even realize it.

As I sit here and write there's a song that comes to my mind that says, *"Wasted years, wasted years oh how foolish. As you walk on in darkness and fear. Turn around, turn around God is calling. He's calling you from a life of wasted years."*

Mom's health was rapidly deteriorating during this time. She was diabetic and was suffering from congestive heart failure and I wasn't making life any easier for her either. In August of 1984, she was so sick the doctors put her in the hospital. She was there for 29 days. On Friday, September 7th she came home. She was so weak she could hardly walk. Saturday morning I went to work up on Smith Mountain Lake. We were building the Vista Pointe Condominiums. About three o'clock that afternoon I told the boys I was going home so I could go see my Mom. When I got within site of the parsonage where my Mom and Dad lived, I saw an ambulance in the front yard. I stopped the car and ran to the house as fast as I could. I went straight to her bedroom, but she wasn't there. When I turned around, my Dad was standing there in the doorway. I asked, "Where's Mom?" He said, "She's in the dining room." When I walked into that room and saw her, I thought my heart would break. She was lying on the floor with a sheet over her. I fell to my knees, picked her up in my arms, and pulled the sheet from her face. I kissed her and told her how much I loved her, but she was gone. I thought about the ugly things I had said to her out of anger. I remember one day she told me that if anything happened to her for me not to go to her funeral looking the way I did. I had long hair and a beard which she despised. I said, "There won't be anything you can do about it if I do because you'll be dead." I told her how sorry I was for that, but it was too late.

Country Music Days

Mom's funeral was on Monday, September 10th, at the Emmanuel Pentecostal Holiness church. I asked Byron if I should get a haircut and shave before going to her funeral. He said, "Mom told you that out of hurt because of the way you are living." I went on to her funeral like I was. I really didn't have time to get a haircut. Although I knew Mom had forgiven me, I still felt so much guilt. After her funeral, we all went back to the parsonage at Swansonville for lunch. The house was so full of people you couldn't find a place to stand, much less sit.

After we ate, I was talking to some of my aunts when Byron came to the door and asked me to come out in the yard. He said he wanted to show me something. When I walked out on the porch my brother Byron and his wife Marinas, my brother Harold and his wife Margie, my sister Lynell and my wife Louise were all standing together in the front yard. Byron was holding a book in his hand. He said they wanted me to read something. My Mom had kept a diary on our family starting back before she and Dad ever got married back in 1946. We have twelve of these scrapbooks that she had written. The book Byron was holding was book number twelve which I had never seen. He opened it up to the last pages Mom had written. It was about Mother's

Day of 1984. After that she was too sick to write anymore. With Byron pastoring, and Harold and Margie being active in their church, it was hard for all the family to get together at one time, but we all came home for Mother's Day that year and took Mom out to eat on Saturday night. We had flowers for her at the restaurant. She wrote about how good it was to have the family together, how beautiful the flowers were, and how good the meal was. Harold and Margie spent the night and went to church at Swansonville on Sunday morning. Byron and Marinas had to get back to Altavista for Sunday services. Harold asked me if I would go to church on Sunday morning so we could sing a song especially for Mom for Mother's Day. I hadn't been to church in a long time, and to be honest, I really didn't want to go because I was afraid I would get under conviction, but I told him I would go. Harold and I sang *The Old Rugged Cross* and dedicated it to Mom. That was one of her favorite songs. Louise and Margie cooked lunch for everybody. Mom wrote about how pretty the song was, how good the meal was, and then I read the last sentence she ever wrote. It said, "I thank God for my family. All I want is for Billy to come back to the Lord." I cannot begin to tell to you what I felt. My heart felt like it had broken into a million pieces. Byron asked me, "Are you ready?" I said, "Yes". Standing there in the front yard on Monday, September 10, 1984 at about 4:30 in the afternoon, with all my family gathered around me, I asked the Lord to forgive me, and to save me, and He did! I can take you to the spot within just a few feet of where it happened. My Dad said, "I just stood there on the porch and watched my children praying." He said, "I felt like a king."

I've had many battles to fight since that day. It's been 26 years and I'm still fighting. Satan doesn't give up or give in, and I guess he never will.

First John 2: 1-2.

My little children, these things write I unto you, that ye sin not. And if any man sin, we have an advocate with the Father, Jesus Christ the righteous; and He is the propitiation for our sins: and not for ours only, but also for the sins of the whole world.

There have been times I stumbled and had to put this scripture to the test, but I found His word to be true. I love the Lord with all my heart and I want to see what's waiting at the end of this Christian journey.

According to my Bible, on September 10, 1984, there went an uproar among the Angels in heaven. They were rejoicing and I believe my Mom looked up and asked, "What was that all about?" I believe the Lord looked at her, and He smiled and said, "Your oldest son just came home."

Oh, and by the way, as for my buddy in Nashville? Well, he went with his wife and two children to church one Sunday morning, he got under conviction, and he got saved. He's now pastoring a church just outside of Nashville. GOD IS SO GOOD!

HOW DID PETER GET BACK TO THE BOAT?

There's a story in the Bible
When Jesus came walking on the sea
The disciples were so afraid
But Peter cried "Lord let me come to thee"
He walked out on the water
Heard the winds and stopped to think
Doubts filled his mind and he started to sink

Don't criticize ole' Peter
For his lack of faith that day
There're still a lot of Christians
Who act the same way
They're fine as long as the way is smooth
And they don't hear a sound

But let the wind start blowing and they cry

"I'm gonna' drown"

Chorus

Have you wondered

How did Peter get back to the boat?

Did he swim or did he float?

I believe when he finally turned his eyes back to the Lord

He went dancing across the waves

And jumped on board

Well you've taken a step out on the sea of life

And Satan says you're gonna' drown

You feel yourself sinking

And you start to thinking

Any minute I'm going down

Turn your eyes to Jesus

That's all you've got to do

And what he did for Peter

He'll do the same for you

Chorus

Have you wondered

How did Peter get back to the boat?

Did he swim or did he float?

I believe when he finally turned his eyes back to the Lord

He went dancing across the waves

And jumped on board

MY STEPMOTHER, FRANCES PARRISH JONES

If I randomly asked ten people, "How long do you think a widow or widower should wait after the death of their spouse to start dating or to get married," I would probably get ten different answers. The truth is, there's no definitive answer. It's up to the individual, and by individual I'm speaking of the widow or widower, not friends, not church members, not family, and not even their own children. Losing your spouse is something one must experience to really understand and to comprehend the void that is left in their heart and life. Thank God it's something I've never experienced, but I got a glimpse of what it's like by being with my Dad when he experienced it. My sister, Lynell, commented to me that she would wake up in the middle of the night and Dad would be sitting at the kitchen table crying like his heart would break.

Outside of our decision to accept the Lord as our Saviour, nothing has the potential to change our lives more than the decision of getting married, be it the first time or second. This is why much time should be spent on our knees in earnest prayer about this life-changing decision.

Not long after the death of our mother, my brothers, my sister, and I were faced with this very question, "How long is long enough and how soon is too soon?" Dad came to us and told us he was talking to a lady and wanted to know what we thought about it. The general consensus was, "If it makes you happy, then it makes us happy. You do what you feel is right for you. Mom is gone and she's not coming back. You have nothing to prove to anyone. You proved your love and devotion to her when she was living, but now you have to go on with your life." It's easy for those who've never had to face this tragedy to tell someone who is facing it what they should or should not do. They can go back to their homes, shut the door and be with their families, but what about those who are alone, perhaps for the first time in their lives?

Now, having said that, I would like to tell you about the most wonderful and the sweetest step-mother anyone could ever wish for.

I was with Daddy the day he officially met Frances Stowe Parrish. He had known of her, but their paths had never crossed. Dad told me, as far as he knew, and the best he could remember, they had never spoken to each other even though they only lived a few miles apart. Her husband, Joe, had passed away about six months before my Mom. During that six month's time, Frances had hired someone to paint the window frames and facings in her house. When the painters put the glass back in the storm windows they didn't install them correctly, and when the wind blew, the windows made a lot of noise. Frances' son, Gary said, "Mom, Preacher Jones installs storm windows. Maybe he can stop by and see what the problem is." When Gary called, my Dad told him, "I don't know when I'll be able to come by. My wife is very sick, but I'll try to come as soon as I can."

After Mom's funeral, I spent as much time with Dad as I possibly could. I went with him to work about every day, and on the days I couldn't go, Byron came down and helped. I remember he had a lot of jobs we had to catch up on. Dad had a lot of contractors waiting for doors and windows. We were very busy for about a month. One day he said, "I need to go by and check some windows for Joe Parrish's widow. Her son called four or five months ago and asked if I would come by and see what the problem was." I said, "Well, let's go." When Nanny came to the door she looked so pretty. (By the way, we've always called her Nanny. I'm not sure how that started, but that's the only thing I ever remember calling her.) Daddy introduced himself first and then me. She said, "I know who you are. I'm Frances, ya'll come on in." That was the beginning of the best thing that could have happened to my Daddy. I remember them talking about how hard it was being alone and not having someone to talk to. I know they had their children they could talk to, but we're talking about something entirely different. We're talking about someone to fill that empty place I spoke of earlier. You cannot convince me that this was not one of those times God was at work behind the scenes.

It took us a good while to look at those windows that day, and naturally Daddy had to go back to finish the job. I wonder why he didn't ask me to go with him? Just today, I was picking at Nanny about checking Daddy out when he was down on his knees working on that window. I remember when she said, "Wait, Brother Jones, let me hold that curtain back so you can see what you're doing." We still laugh about that, but of course, I have to embellish it just a little bit. I told her, "I saw you looking down at him and licking your lips." She gets the biggest laugh out of that.

Well, it wasn't long before we were planning a wedding. On June 29, 1985, Byron performed the ceremony and Lynell, Louise and I sang for their wedding. It was the sweetest ceremony. I was so happy for them.

Whenever we went by to see Daddy and Nanny, we knew what they would probably be doing, studying their Sunday School lessons. They both taught a class at the Emmanuel Pentecostal Holiness Church. I wouldn't hesitate one minute to say they put at least five to six hours a week on their lessons and maybe more. There's one word that comes to my mind when I think about Daddy and Nanny, and that's "Faithful." They worked as hard, if not harder, on their Sunday School lesson, as a lot of preachers do on their sermons.

I must say how wonderful Nanny's children, Billy, Gary, Joann and Steve have been to Byron, Harold, Lynell, David and me. Not once have we ever had any kind of problem or disagreement. They have been nothing but kind to us, and I think they would say the same about us. They were so good to my Daddy.

Daddy and Nanny had fifteen wonderful years together. They took trips to The Holy Land, Yellowstone National

Park, The Amish Country, Florida and they even went to Hawaii with Billy and his wife, Linda.

On August 22, 2000, we stood by Daddy's hospital bed and sang, "Leaning On The Everlasting Arms," as he left this world. I want to say "thank you" to Nanny for making my Daddy's last fifteen years happy years. I remember when it was my night to sit with him at the hospital. He would wake up all during the night wanting to know if his sweetie was there yet. Nanny, he loved you very much, and I know you loved him as well.

Since Dad's death, we decided to step back a little, not because we don't love Nanny, but she has her children, grandchildren and great-grandchildren, and we don't want to impose in any way on them. Nanny, I just want you to know, we still love you and appreciate you so very, very much. I'm so proud to call you my stepmother.

CALLED TO BE FAITHFUL

Some are called to preach
Some are called to teach
And some to a foreign land
But there is one call
That goes out to all
Who've knelt at Calvary
And placed their hearts
And lives in God's hands

Faithful, we're called to be Faithful
To the task we've been asked to do
It may never be seen by man
Still it's part of God's perfect plan
He has called us so we must be Faithful

There is work for all to do,
My friend this includes you
If your sins are under the blood
It's not by works, we are saved by grace
Still we must stand up and take our place
Precious souls are dying without God

Faithful, we're called to be Faithful
To the task we've been asked to do
It may never be seen by man
Still it's part of God's perfect plan
He has called us we must be Faithful

Then on that Day we'll hear Him say
Well done my child
Enter into the joys of the Lord
Faithful, I found you Faithful
Come on in my child
Welcome home my child
The victory's won my child
You have been Faithful
I found you Faithful

THE DAY OUR LIVES CHANGED FOREVER

O f all the things I've wanted to write about or felt I should write about, this is by far the most dreaded and the most difficult. When we wake up in the mornings, we think we have a pretty good idea of what we would like to accomplish on that particular day, but it doesn't always turn out like we plan. Sometimes, all it takes is just one phone call to change not only our plans for the day, but the potential is there to change our lives forever. Such was our day, Wednesday, March 1, 1995.

Louise, Angel and I had just moved back to Dry Fork, Virginia to be closer to my Dad and to our church. It was fifty-five miles from where we were living to our church at Swansonville and about the same to my Dad's. Louise had accepted a job as the Plant Manager's secretary at Times Fiber and Cable Company in Chatham, Virginia. I was self employed, hanging and finishing drywall. Louise had left for work that morning, and as always, she dropped Angel off at the Tot Spot Day Care Center in Chatham. I was doing a remodeling job about a mile or two from home. I guess I had been on the job maybe an hour or so that morning when I heard a car horn blowing. I remember asking someone, "Who is making all that noise outside?" Finally, I looked out the window and it was my pastor, Rev. Mike Hearp and his wife, Judy. I opened the window to see what was going on and he motioned for me to come out to the car. I remember putting my tools down and running down the steps and out the door. I knew something must be wrong. When I got there Judy had moved to the back seat and I noticed she was crying. I asked, "What in the world is going on?" Mike told me to sit down, he had some bad news. I sat down in the front seat and Mike said, "I don't know exactly how to tell you this, but Louise's Mother and Daddy are both dead." That alone was hard enough to accept, but when he began to tell me what had happened, it was unbelievable. There's no way you can prepare anyone for news like this. He told me that Louise's sister, Annette, had just called. Early that morning, their Dad shot their mother, and then turned the gun on himself. The first thing that came to my mind was, "How am I going to tell Louise?" I will never forget that seven mile trip to Chatham. I kept asking myself, "How am I going to be able to do this?" Brother Mike told me it would be best not to tell her anything until I got her to the car. When we got there Mike parked as close to the front door as he possibly could. When you go in the front door at her workplace, you walk into a waiting room. There is a phone you use to tell the receptionist who you are and what your purpose is for being there. The receptionist was on break, so Louise picked up. She said, "What in the world are you doing here?" About that time she pressed the buzzer to unlock the door so I could go into her office. Again she asked me what I needed. I said, "I need you to go with me out to the car, we need to talk." She said, "I can't, I'm at work. I can't just walk out." I said, "Honey, we need to talk, but we can't talk in here. Get your coat and pocket book and let's go outside." She started crying and asked, "What's wrong with Angel?" I told her Angel was fine there was nothing wrong with her. She kept saying, "Please tell me what's wrong." I said, "I will when we get outside." When she went to get her coat I stepped into the Plant Manager's office and told him what had happened. He told me to take all the time she needed. When we walked out the door and she saw Mike and Judy, she went all to pieces. She kept begging, "Please tell me what's wrong," but I couldn't. I was afraid she would pass out. When she sat down in the back seat beside Judy, I knelt down beside her in the doorway of the car. I said, "Honey, you know your Mom and Dad have been sick for a long time and it's been hard on your Dad. This morning, he shot your Mom and then he shot himself. They are both dead." She started screaming, "No, my Daddy wouldn't do that, my Daddy wouldn't do that!" I've never felt so helpless in my life. What do you say or do at a time like that? All I could do was hold her.

Mike and Judy took us straight home so we could pack and get on the road. We had a four hour drive to Newport News, Virginia. We had no idea how long we would be gone so we had to make sure we had enough clothes. We picked Angel up from daycare on our way out of town. Louise tried her best to keep her composure for Angel's sake, but there were times she completely lost control. Angel was three years old so she was very much aware something was wrong. She kept asking, "Mommy, what's the matter?" Louise just told her she wasn't feeling well.

I had mixed feelings about our arrival at Annette's house. I was glad the trip was over, but I dreaded the reunion. It happened pretty much like I thought it would. It broke my heart to see them hurting the way they were. Annette is the oldest of the four children. Charlie (Buck) is next, then Allen, who has passed away since then. Louise is the baby. Being the youngest she was the apple of her Daddy's eye. His pet name for her was Lucy. He never called her Louise.

Mike and Judy came down the next day. My sister, Lynell, rode with them. My Dad and my step-mother, Frances, were planning to come down later on that same day, but while in town taking care of some business that morning, an elderly man ran a stop light and hit them broad side. It banged both of them up pretty bad so they were unable to come down for the funerals. We had the receiving of friends on Friday night and the funerals were on Saturday morning at 11:00. Rev. L. H. Garner, Louise's former pastor and our pastor, Rev. Mike Hearp conducted the funerals. What do people do at a time like this without a church family, a pastor, and especially without the Lord?

Mike and Judy were so wonderful and helpful to us. We didn't have to worry about Angel at all. Sister Judy gave her the best of care. As usual, Mike wanted to pitch in and help wherever he could. I don't know what we would have done without them.

I want it to be known, my father-in-law, Charles T. West, Sr. was not a mean or violent man. He loved his family. He was a good husband for 54 years, a good father, a good grandfather, and a fantastic father-in-law. I remember when we would go home for a visit he would buy T-bone steaks and grill them outside. I always stayed outside with him while he cooked the steaks. He would say, "Taste this, it's really good." He would cut off the tender part of the T-bone and give it to me. Then he would say, "This will be our secret." By the time we got ready to eat I was already full, but I always managed to eat more.

Louise's Daddy was a very sick 73 year old man. Her mother was 67 years old and had suffered several strokes, which left her partially paralyzed and she had a heart condition. She would get her days and nights mixed up and would wake up at 2:00 in the morning wanting a cup of coffee. He was up and down all night, every night, trying to take care of her. The children had tried to get them to move to an assisted living facility but Edna Earl King West would not hear of it. I can tell you right now, nobody made her do anything she didn't want to do. She was a very strong-willed person. As a matter of fact Louise's brother, Charlie, has a goat with that same type personality. Guess what he named it? Yep, you're right, Edna Earl.

Louise's Daddy had some demons he had been fighting for most of his adult life. What he did that morning he didn't do out of anger, but rather out of desperation, and I believe out of love. He just couldn't deal with it anymore. He did the only thing he knew to do. Mama and Papa (That's what the grand kids called them) hardly ever went to church, but they always made sure the children had a way if they wanted to go.

Several months before all this took place Louise and I got home from work one afternoon and I told her I couldn't get her Daddy off my mind. I had a burden for him and really needed to talk to him. She said, "Well, let's go down there." I said, "I feel like I need to." We jumped in the car and made the trip to Newport News. It was probably 8:00 or 8:30 when we got there. When we walked in the door her Mom was sitting in her chair in the living room. She said, "What in the world are ya'll doing here? Why didn't you call and tell us you were coming?" Louise said, "It was a spur of the moment decision. Billy needs to talk to Daddy. Is he here?" She said, "Yes, he's in his room watching the ball game." When I opened the door and he saw me, the biggest smile you ever saw came across his face. He said, "Boy, what in the world are you doing here?" I said, "Papa, I've come to tell you something." He looked at me with a puzzled look on his face and said, "What?" I said, "The Lord wants me to tell you that he loves you and he wants to save you." He looked at me and the biggest tears you've ever seen started flowing down his face. About that time a commercial came on the TV. They were advertising a gospel record by the Statler Brothers. They started singing, "Just as I am without one plea but that thy blood was shed for me." Now folks, that was not by coincidence. That was orchestrated by Almighty God. I said, "Papa, don't you want to be saved?" He shook his head yes and I asked, "Do you want to pray right now?" And again he said, "Yes." We started praying, but he wasn't saying anything, so I stopped and said, "Papa, you need to talk to the Lord and tell Him what you want." He said, "I did and He just saved me." We were both crying and I said, "Papa, do you want to tell Louise?" He shook his head yes. I yelled, "Honey, come in here, your Daddy wants to tell you something!" When she walked in the room he grabbed her in his arms and said, "Lucy, the Lord just saved me."

I don't know what his state of mind was the morning of March 1, 1995. It's not for me or anyone else to judge. I'm going to leave that to a merciful, loving, and all-knowing God.

Sometimes things happen in our lives that have the potential to totally destroy us, but for the grace of God. We have no idea what tomorrow holds for us, but I'm so thankful I know who holds tomorrow. As the song writer said;

I don't know about tomorrow
I just live from day to day
I don't borrow from its sunshine
For its skies may turn to gray
I don't worry o'er the future
For I know what Jesus said
And today I'll walk beside Him
For He knows what is ahead

Many things about tomorrow
I don't seem to understand
But I know who holds tomorrow
And I know who holds my hand

If you don't know the Lord Jesus Christ as your personal Savior, I invite you to ask Him into your heart right now. It's not hard at all. Why don't you pray this prayer with me?

Lord Jesus, I am a sinner and I realize if I were to die right now I would be lost. I ask you as sincerely as I know how to forgive me and to cleanse me from my sins and from all unrighteousness. Write my name in your Lambs Book of Life. I accept you as my Lord and my Savior. Thank you for saving me. Amen.

Just reading these words won't save you, but if you prayed this prayer from the depths of your heart, my friend, according to my Bible, you are forgiven. You are SAVED! If you prayed this prayer and accepted the Lord as your Savior I would love to hear from you. You can contact me at: billyihavebeensaved@gmail.com

NO! THIS CANNOT BE HAPPENING TO ME

ॐ

The date was Thursday, August, 29, 2002. I was out mowing the grass when I started experiencing severe chest pains. I tried to finish mowing, but the pain was so intense I had to try to make it back to the house. We had eaten lasagna at an Italian restaurant that evening, so I thought I knew what the problem was. When I finally made it to the house, I asked Louise if we had any Rolaids or Tums. She asked me what was wrong. I told her I had severe indigestion, so she gave me some Rolaids. I chewed them up and then laid down on the couch for a little while. After about an hour it eased off, so I went back outside to finish mowing. I hadn't been out there very long when it hit me again. The pain was so severe and intense I found it very difficult to breathe. I left the mower where it was, and when I made it back to the house I took some more Rolaids and laid down again. For several hours the pain would come and go, but it finally became so severe I couldn't take it anymore. Angel went back to the bedroom and said, "Mommy, Dad must really be hurting bad because he's moaning really loud." Angel was only ten years old, but she knew something was wrong. We called Tara Cobbs who went to our church and was a nurse at the hospital. I told her what my symptoms were and that I thought it was just acid reflux or indigestion. I knew it couldn't be my heart because I had just had a stress test done the month before. Tara said, "Tell Louise to get you to the hospital as fast as she can. I work third shift and I'm leaving for work right now. I'll come by the ER and check on you." I think she wanted us to call the rescue squad, but I didn't want to bother them for nothing.

There weren't very many laws that Louise didn't break while trying to get me to the hospital. About half way there the pain went away, so I told her to turn around and go back home. She said, "I am not," and continued on to the hospital.

When we got to the emergency room, they rushed me in and started all kinds of tests. None of the tests indicated that there was a problem, so they were going to send me back home. When they called the heart doctor, he said, "Keep him overnight. I've got to be there first thing in the morning to do a catheterization on another patient. I'll look in on him then." After they put me in a room Louise and Angel went back home. The next morning the nurse brought my breakfast to me and said, "The doctor should be in any time." I finished my breakfast and about that time the doctor walked in. He looked at my test results and said they looked pretty good, but something wasn't right. He told the nurses to prep me for a catheterization. Even though the nurse told him I had eaten breakfast, he said, "I have a strange feeling about this, so go ahead and prep him." I asked them to please wait until my wife got there and they said, "We'll wait as long as we can." I also asked them if I could call my pastor. If I remember correctly I believe Brother Mike, my pastor, got there before Louise. Finally, they said they couldn't wait any longer and took me on back.

Louise and Angel had stopped to eat breakfast that morning. Then Louise took Angel to Day Care before coming on to the hospital. I had called her earlier that morning and told her to take her time. I had not had any pain since the night before and the doctor was going to check me and then I could go home. When she got there she couldn't believe they had taken me back for a catheterization.

I remember laying there watching the monitor. I could see the wire inching its way through the veins and then all of a sudden there was silence and then whispers. I heard the doctor whisper to the two nurses, "Stay with him and don't leave him," then he left the room. The nurses stood there and talked to me until he came back. They kept asking me, "How are you feeling? Are you in any pain?" When he walked back in the room he came straight to me and said, "You're going to be taking a trip today." I remember asking him, "Where am I going?" He said, "The helicopter is on its way from Duke. You've got to have emergency bypass surgery today." I thought, "No, this cannot be happening to me, not this physically, robust specimen of manhood." (You were suppose to laugh right there.) The first thing I said was, "I want to see my wife." When Louise came in the room Brother Mike was with her. The doctor had already talked to them before he told me. I will never forget the look on her face. She grabbed my hand and didn't want to let go. They took me to ICU to wait for the helicopter. The doctor told me not to raise my head off the pillow and to lie perfectly still.

Lynell had arrived and Louise asked her to go get Angel and take her home to help pack a suitcase. She said, "Angel will know where to find everything I need. I'm going to get on the road so I'll be there before he goes to surgery. When you come down bring my suitcase with you." In the meantime they called Byron and Harold and told them what was going on. It wasn't long before they were all headed to Duke.

While I was in ICU, I heard the helicopter circle over the hospital. It seemed like it took forever for them to get from the landing pad to the hospital. They had to unload all their equipment from the helicopter into an ambulance, drive two blocks to the hospital, switch me from the hospital monitoring equipment to theirs, which took forever, and then take me back to the helicopter. Louise, Brother Mike, and Lynell had all left so they could get to Duke as quickly as possible. When they were ready to take me to the landing pad, it so happened that the Dry Fork Rescue Squad was about to leave the hospital, so they asked them if they would mind transporting me to the helicopter. Needless to say I was very nervous and apprehensive about all that was going on. I had never had anyone make that much fuss over me in my life. It was all so sudden, and after all I just had indigestion, so I thought. The worst part of all, I didn't know if I would ever see my family again. When they backed up to the helicopter to transfer me, I looked up and I saw a familiar face. Frank Dolan looked down at me and said, "I didn't know it was you we were transporting." Frank is the Chief of the Dry Fork Volunteer Fire Department and lives down the road from us. Just seeing somebody I knew really helped.

I had always wanted to ride in a helicopter, but not lying down. I really preferred to see where I was going. All I could see was a nurse at my feet, and one at my head, monitoring my vitals. The trip didn't take but twenty minutes. When they rolled me into the emergency room, two men with razors attacked my chest with the vigor of two chickens on a June bug. I asked them, "Where's the shaving cream?" They said, "There's no time for that." At that moment they were inflicting more pain on me with those razors than my heart was.

The rest is very blurry because they had me sedated on all kinds of medication. I do remember them letting Louise, Lynell, and my brother Harold in to see me just before going to surgery. Louise asked if Brother Mike could come in and have prayer, but they said there was no more time. They were waiting for me in the operating room. Louise kissed me and then they took me to the operating room. I can still see those tears running down her face.

My surgery lasted into the early hours of Saturday morning, August 31st. I had a total of seven blockages with the main artery 99% blocked. I was a time bomb about to explode. I could go into a lot more detail, but I'll spare you. As far as I know, I don't have an enemy in this world, but if I did, I wouldn't wish this on them.

When they finally took me from ICU to a regular room the doctor who did my surgery came in to check on me. I will never forget when he said to me, "The only reason you're still alive is because God is not finished with you yet." He went on to say, "I've never seen that much blockage in a living person before." It was very humbling to hear a doctor tell me that. I asked him if I actually had a heart attack and his response was, "Technically, yes, but there was no damage done to your heart muscles. God was watching over you. You got here just in time. You were on the verge of a massive heart attack."

You may be asking yourself, "Why in the world is he writing about having open heart surgery?" Well, the answer is very simple. There are actually two reasons. First, I have so much to be thankful for. If Tara had not told me to go straight to the hospital, I wouldn't be here today. If my wife had listened to me and gone back home instead of going on to the hospital, I wouldn't be here today. If Dr. Zakhary had not told the ER doctors to keep me overnight, I wouldn't be here today, and if Dr. Zakhary had not done the catheteriza-tion, I wouldn't be here today. But most of all, if not for the mercy and grace of God, I wouldn't be here today. I've got so much to be thankful for.

There is a second reason I wanted to write about this. I feel a need to warn anyone and everyone who finds them-selves in this same dilemma, to please call 911 immediately. Don't try to do your own diagnosis. Even if the pain goes away, you go to the hospital anyway. We hear of young people in their twenties and thirties having heart attacks, so please seek help immediately. Learn the symptoms of a heart attack. Your experience could be completely different from mine. I thought it was the spices and seasoning in my food, but I was wrong. Life is too precious and fragile to be handled so frivolously. Oh, and by the way, I did say I was writing about unforgettable moments in my life. Trust me, this is about as unforgettable as it gets.

What I'm about to share with you now is the most impor-tant thing of all. If you don't know Jesus as the Lord and Savior of your life, then I beg of you, make things right with Him, because when you look at your life from an eternal per-spective, what else really matters? We can go to heaven as a result of having a physically sick heart, but not a spiritually or a sin sick heart. The best decision you could ever make is to first, invite Jesus into your heart and life, and then take care of your physical heart. After all, don't you think that's what God expects us to do?

Rev. & Mrs. Michael Elwood Hearp

THAT'S JUST THE WAY HE IS

I would like to tell you about one of the most unusual and special people I've ever known. Mike Hearp is not only my Pastor, but he's also my best friend. Mike has been my

Pastor for the past 25 years. I treat him like he's my brother, and he treats me like I'm his brother. We can be totally honest with one another and let our hair down with one another (that is figuratively speaking) yet, not offend one another. Best of all, in the end, we still love one another. Not only is he the best Pastor anyone could ever ask for, wish for, or even hope for, he is also the best friend anyone could ever have. By the way, he will not be given the opportunity to read this until it has been published, because he will adamantly object. These are my personal thoughts and feelings and are in no way an attempt to defend him, because he needs no defending. It is, however, an attempt to bestow honor, appreciation and gratitude on one who is very much deserving. Let me quickly point out, that when I say Mike, this automatically includes his wife, Sister Judy, because they are a team. Now where was I? Oh yes, Mike is always there when you need him and some folks might say, "If you need him or not, he's always there." He instinctively knows what to say, how to say it, and when to say it, and he also knows what to do, how to do it, and when it should be done. He has been accused of trying to do too much, but THAT'S JUST THE WAY HE IS. He sees a need and feels that it's his moral obligation and responsibility to fill that need. He has the uncanny ability to use humor to lighten what may be considered a very tense or emotional situation or moment. His wisdom far exceeds his years, although his years are rapidly catching up with his wisdom. (This is going to end up being a very close and interesting race.) I think it's probably the reading glasses perched on the end of his nose that gives him the appearance of, "The wise old man." But, of course, the bald head and gray hair around the sides help a lot also.

If I approached not only members of our church, but people in general whose lives have been touched by Mike and Judy Hearp, and I asked them to share what Mike and Judy have meant to them and their families, it would take volumes to contain it all. Times, such as the death of a loved one, or a time of sickness, or even during happy times such as weddings, birthdays, anniversaries, or just family gatherings, they are always there. (Now Brother Hearp, I'm telling the truth so you stop shaking your head. I'm writing this and I can verify every word of it.) I know him like a book. Sometimes you just have to get rough on him. He doesn't mind giving accolades to others, and doing for others, and bestowing honor on others, but he's very uncomfortable with receiving it for himself. Honestly, he would rather be helping someone move than to publicly receive any kind of honor or accolades for himself. (Now, he's shaking his head yes. I told you I know him like a book.) The fact of the matter is, most of what he does is done in secret, and not many people, if any, know anything about it. But, that's the way he wants it. I've shared a number of things he's done for me and my family in other stories in this book, but I left some details out such as, when he took our car and filled it up with gas while we were packing to go to Newport News, Virginia for Louise's Mom and Dad's funerals. We didn't know where he had gone. He just got in our car and disappeared. Another time he reserved Louise a room close to the hospital when I had emergency by-pass surgery. I was unaware of this until recently. I was in another world at that time. Most of the time when he does an act of kindness, it comes out of his own pocket, but whether he pays for it or not is not what's most important. It's the fact that he is considerate enough to look ahead and see the need. But, THAT'S JUST THE WAY HE IS. Another time, he and Judy allowed Louise and me to stay with them for a couple of weeks after the birth of our daughter, Angel. According to the adoption laws of the state of Virginia, we could not take Angel out of the state for two weeks after she was born. We were living in North Carolina at that time. Mike and Judy wouldn't say so, but I know it was an inconvenience for them. I could go on and on, but I think you get the picture. Yes, I'm sure there have been times when people have taken advantage of him because of his generosity and kindness, but you won't hear him complain. THAT'S JUST THE WAY HE IS.

There's one last thing that I feel needs to be said. If you ever hear anyone make a derogatory remark or say anything unkind about Mike because they thought he was unkind, or spoke unkindly, or mistreated them in someway, they either misunderstood what was said or done, or they're just telling their side of the story, or they are being untruthful. Some people mistake firmness and standing for what's right as being rude or unkind, but that's not true. First of all, Mike is not the kind of person to intentionally do anything to offend or hurt anyone. Now, he will take a stand for what is right, he will tell you the truth, and he will preach the truth, and if that offends you, then so be it. I know for a fact that if he ever spoke or acted unkindly, he wouldn't get half-way down the street before he would turn around and go back to apologize. Actually, he wouldn't make it out the door because his conscience would bother him until everything was made right. We all know that's the way to keep our conscience tender and sensitive, don't we? If we don't go back and make things right when our conscience tells us we should, eventually we will come to the point we can't hear our conscience when it speaks to us. That could be what some call, "Hard-Hearted," or having no conscience. Mike has never been unkind or rude to me in any way, shape, form or fashion, but he has called to apologize when he thought he might have, just to make sure. THAT'S JUST THE WAY HE IS. Again this is not meant to defend him, for he needs no defending. His character and reputation does that for him. Again these are my thoughts, opinions and feelings and this is my book and it's about unforgettable moments in my life. I consider my friendship with Rev. Michel Elwood Hearp to be unforgettable and yes, even precious.

I've said it once, and I'll say it again. A pulpit does for Mike Hearp what a phone booth did for Clark Kent. He is a totally different person when he steps behind that sacred desk. Mike is a fun loving, happy person who enjoys having a good time, but when it comes to preaching the word of God and ministering to the hearts of people and taking a stand for the truth, it's all serious business. He learned a long time ago, it's not his business, but it's his Father's business, and we all must be about our Father's business. THAT'S JUST THE WAY HE IS.

MY DAD
REV. WILLIE BENNETT JONES
(BILLY JONES)

Not only was W. B. Jones (Billy Jones) my Daddy, but he was my hero and my inspiration. He was the best example I've ever seen of how one should live and conduct himself, day in and day out. I know, most all sons probably feel that way about their Dads, but I don't say this just because he was my Dad. I say it because of his character and his commitment, not only to his wife and children, but his commitment to God and to the ministry. He was committed to living right, doing right, acting right, and talking right. I've never heard my Dad use any kind of foul language in my life. Not many people can say that of their Dad. My Dad was not a rich man by any stretch of the imagination. He worked hard all his life to provide for his family, most of the time just barely scraping by.

When Dad was in the 10th grade, he quit high school to work on the farm. About a year later he was drafted into the Army during WWII. Upon returning home after the war, he met my mother. They fell in love and got married December 20, 1946. One night at a revival at Oakland Methodist Church, he stood up and announced that the Lord had called him to preach. He went back to Whitmel Farm Life School and finished high school. After a few detours, he ended up at Holmes Bible College. I had the privilege of going to his high school graduation and his college graduation. Right after college he took his first church as pastor of the Bethel Pentecostal Holiness Church.

Sometimes, Daddy had what might be considered, a funny or strange way of getting his point across, but nevertheless he got it across. I remember on one occasion I was upset about something that someone had said or done, and I was talking about what I was going to do about it. Dad looked at me and without cracking a smile he spoke these very words, "Son, the more you stir a dog pile, the worse it stinks, so leave it alone." You may not care for the visual this illustration presents, but nevertheless he got his point across loud and clear. Don't worry. He never used that expression in a sermon or outside the family.

I've never seen my Dad lose his temper. Well, not with other people anyway, but he had three sons who on many occasions pushed his patience to the limit and beyond. It was the beyond part that caused pain to be inflicted on our behind part. I remember that leather strap very well. It was actually a belt, but we wore it more than he did if you know what I mean. Each time before putting it to use, he would say, "Son, this is going to hurt me more than it hurts you." That's the only time I've ever felt there was the remote possibility my Dad could be lying.

There are so many things I could share with you about my Dad. If Byron, Harold, and Lynell were here we could go on and on with stories about him. There are some things that need to be told for posterity reasons, if for no other. One such story was when Dad was pastoring the Bethel Pentecostal Holiness Church. He and Mom had gone to Howdy Dillard's Store to pick up a few groceries. (I just found out recently that it was actually called Hallie Dillard's Store. I guess as kids we got it mixed up with Howdy Doody.) It was just a few miles up the road, so they left us at home. When they returned, Dad told us there was a bad wreck up the road and

145

he wanted us to see it. On the way there, he explained to us that the driver of the car was drinking. He said, "Boys, this is what happens when people drink alcohol." He went on to explain to us the evils of alcohol and that it was a sin. He really drove that message home. When we got there, Dad pulled off the road and we walked up to where the wreck was. The car was upside down in the middle of the road. Dad made sure we stayed a safe distance away. About that time a car pulled up to where we were standing. The man driving asked Daddy if he would drive his car past where the State Troopers were because he was drunk and didn't want them to see him. For obvious reasons Dad told him no and we walked a little closer to the wreck. There was gasoline running all across the road from the wrecked car. About that time that drunk driver went by and when he did, he flipped a cigarette out the window and it landed in the gasoline. Someone yelled, "Get back, it's going to explode." My Daddy ran over and grabbed the cigarette. A lot of people could have been injured or killed if it had not been for my Dad's quick actions. It was the mercies of God that kept the gasoline from igniting. He never received any kind of acknowledgement or accolades for what he did, but he was a hero in our eyes.

My Dad never pastored a full-time church. He always worked a job to help support his family while pastoring, but let it be known, the ministry held top priority in his life. For about twenty-five years, he installed storm windows and doors to help supplement his income. By working for himself he had control of his time and schedule. In his early ministry he sold cars, sold building material, sold pots and pans, worked in factories, anything he could find to help pay the bills.

My Dad was very conscientious and very careful not to put himself in any kind of situation that would bring his character into question. I remember on one occasion he had to go quite a ways out in the country to put windows and doors on a house for an elderly couple. Their daughter lived in Gretna where we lived. She told Daddy, "When you go to put the windows and doors on my Mom and Dad's house, I want to ride with you." I'll never forget the night before he was to install those windows and doors, he said, "Boys, I don't care which one of you it is, but one of you will be sitting between me and that lady tomorrow morning." At that time I thought it was silly making us go with him, but as I grew older I realized why. He was protecting his good name and his ministry from being tarnished by rumors. He was so wise.

Daddy did a lot of ministry while out working. He had the opportunity to sow seeds in the hearts of people who wouldn't darken the doors of a church. He was told on many occasions, "You work harder than any preacher I ever saw. You don't mind getting your hands dirty out here with the working man." He ministered day and night in some way, form or fashion. I've seen him come home from work, take a bath, grab a bite to eat and take off to the hospital, or go visit someone who was sick, or go to the funeral home. This wasn't just once in a while, but it was at least two or three times a week. There have been many, many times I've heard my Daddy and Mama say, "Boys, you're on your own for supper tonight. Someone is sick and we've got to go." We were used to that. We stayed home and kept our baby sister, Lynell, while they went to help someone else. For example, I remember Sister Margaret Yeatts who went to our church in Gretna. She had two hospital beds in her home. Her mother-in-law, Mrs. Yeatts, was in one, and her husband, John, was in the other. She was back and forth between the two taking care of them day and night. Mom and Dad spent a lot of time helping her. John had throat cancer. The doctors told Sister Margaret it would eventually eat through his jugular vein and he would bleed to death. That's exactly what happened. John died early in the morning hours. Mom and Dad had been there all night helping Sister Margaret. Daddy held him in his arms and prayed as he died. It was a comforting thing for Daddy to know that just a few short months prior to this, he had the privilege of leading John to the Lord. John had been told by another minister that he was saved and had nothing to worry about, but he told my Dad that he knew he wasn't. Daddy prayed with him and the Lord saved him.

My goodness, where do I stop? There's so much I could tell you, but I have to draw the line somewhere. There is one funny story I want to tell you though. This took place in Gretna also. The church had built a new fellowship hall and it was close to being finished. They decided to cover the concrete floor with what is called a seamless floor covering. It consisted of a thick liquid which is poured on the floor. Then there were different colors of chips that you sprinkled on this liquid to create any color floor you desired. After drying for two or three days, you had a beautiful, durable, seamless floor. My dad told the church that he would put the new floor covering down. Dad was famous for reading the directions or instructions after all else failed. On the cans that the liquid came in were labels that read, "Use this product only in well ventilated spaces." It was on a Wednesday when Dad put the new flooring down. About two hours before prayer meeting, Daddy pulled into the yard at home. When he got out of his truck, he was staggering, and laughing, and giggling. When Mom saw him it really scared her because she didn't know what was wrong. She later said, "I've never seen him drunk before." Finally, when he was able to explain what had happened, he told Mom there wasn't enough ventilation and the fumes from the floor were very, very strong. He said, "I sure am glad the police didn't stop me on the way home," and he burst out laughing. Then he said, "Somebody help me upstairs, I've got to get ready for church," and again he burst out laughing. Everything was funny to him. Mom said, "You're not going anywhere, especially to church. You're going straight to bed. I'll preach tonight." Then she said, "How do I tell the church folks you were too drunk to go to church?" Then she started laughing. As far as I know he never put down another seamless floor.

I've seen my Dad take all kinds of verbal abuse from church members and church board members. It didn't happen often, but nevertheless, it did happen. Although I remember it, I can honestly say I have no ill feelings towards anyone, but how do you forget your Dad coming home from a board meeting and laying his head on his desk and crying as though his heart was breaking, all because of the way he was talked to and treated by Christians or should I say, "So-called Christians." I've seen church members get mad and stomp out of church while calling my Dad names, all because a vote didn't go the way they wanted it to. He took it without saying a word. Once when I was away from the Lord, Louise and I went to visit Mom and Dad and went to church with them. There was a man who sat behind my Mom, Lynell and David, and he would make all kinds of derogatory comments about my Dad right out loud while he was preaching. Mom had warned us about it. It so happened that Louise and I were sitting in front of him. It was all I could do to keep from inviting him outside for a pow-wow. You just don't do that to my Daddy.

It doesn't surprise me at the number of preachers' children who do not, and will not, go to church. Although there's no excuse for it, I understand why. It's all because they remember the way their Dad was treated by church people. But I, like so many others, have seen enough good things from good people who didn't have their own agenda, who were not power hungry for control, but they wanted to see the church go forward and grow. We do know that winning souls is called growth, don't we?

If you ever find yourself not in agreement with a minister or someone else in the church, or with what may have been proposed, there are proper steps and channels that can be taken to let your feelings be known. But we must remember, we are one person with one voice or vote. If things don't go the way we think they should then we must accept it as God's will. After all, it's not my church, their church, or your church. It's God's church, and He will build His church. What we do or say must be done and said in the right spirit, and in the right way or we could be guilty of causing harm to the body of Christ. I don't think anyone wants to be guilty of that.

On August 15, 2000, Rev. Mike Hearp and his wife, Judy, and a group of us took our church van and went to the Raleigh-Durham Airport to meet my sister, Lynell. She flew in late that night from China. We got back to Danville about 2:00 in the morning, but even at that late hour we had to go by the hospital to see daddy. He had been there for several weeks. I had been telling him that his girl was coming home that day and he was so anxious to see her. Oh, how he loved his one and only daughter. Lynell had been in China for three months teaching English and doing missions work. While she was there I kept her posted on Daddy's condition. On

Tuesday, August 22nd, one week to the day after she returned home, we stood by his bed and sang to him as he left this world and went to be with the Lord. As I watched him take his last breath I thought to myself, "Oh Daddy, how I wish I could see your face as you walk through those Gates and view the City that I've heard you preach about all my life." I am so grateful that Lynell made it home to be with him before he died. We miss him and long for the day when we will see him again.

Earlier, I made the statement that my Dad was not a rich man by any stretch of the imagination. Well, I think I'll retract that statement. You decide for yourself. As for me, I think my Dad was and is the wealthiest man I've ever known. I'd like to leave you with this poem.

Mom, Dad & Me

BILLY AND ANNA'S OLDEST BOY

I may never be rich or famous

Not that I really want to be

My name may never become

A household word or

Go down in history

But there is one thing

I hold claim to

And it fills my heart with joy

That's when I hold my head high,

And I smile and say

I'm Billy and Anna's oldest boy!

**My Mom and Dad
Rev. & Mrs. W. B. Jones**

IN LOVING MEMORY OF MY MOM "ANNA OAKES JONES"

This book is in memory of the one person who has had the biggest influence on my life besides my Dad. That person is my precious mother, "Anna Oakes Jones" who was born November 20, 1927 and called home to Heaven on September 8, 1984.

It's a miracle Mom lived long enough to see her first full day of life, much less the fifty-six years that she was given. She was born at home and weighed less than two pounds. She had already lost five sisters who were also born prematurely. They kept her in one of her Daddy's shoe boxes. Mom was the youngest of six children. Her oldest sister, Aunt Ola, once told me about my great grandmother putting her wedding band on Moms arm right after she was born and it went all the way up to her shoulder. She also told me about the time they lost her in the bed covers. Everyone had to gather around the bed and carefully lift the covers so she wouldn't fall out on the floor. It is a miracle she lived, but God had plans for her life.

When Mom was seven years old she wanted a pair of black patent leather shoes. One morning before going to school, her Dad told her to stand on a piece of cardboard. He took a pencil and drew around her foot. When she got home that afternoon, she had a pair of black patent leather shoes just like she wanted. She told me, "The first place I wore those shoes was to my Daddy's funeral." My grandfather died just a few days later of a heart attack at the age of 46.

My Dad told me the first time he ever kissed my mother was the night he asked her to marry him. Things sure have changed. Now days they are kissing before they even know each other's name. He would laugh and say, if the passenger door on his truck had come open, she would have fallen out because she sat as close to it as she possibly could. Mom and Dad got married December 20, 1946 and I was born November 1, 1947. I know what you're doing, but that's OK. Go ahead and count.

Mom was not the kind of person to say, "I can't." Whenever she was asked to lend a helping hand or asked to do something she would always say, "I'll try." An example of this was when my Dad first started pastoring. He scheduled Aunt Katie Campbell to come hold a revival at the Bethel Pentecostal Holiness Church. Everyone who knew Sister Campbell called her, "Aunt Katie." There were only about fifteen people attending the church then and none of them could play the piano, so they had to sing with no music. Aunt Katie said, "Sister Jones, why don't you play the piano?" Mom said, "I don't know how. I only know a few chords. I can't play any songs." Aunt Katie said, "That's a lot more than anybody else knows. You just do the best you can and God will help you." For the next two years Mom was the pianist. The Lord blessed her efforts and she became a good pianist. Not long after Junior and Lorene Mitchell got saved, Mom and Sister Lorene started singing duets together with Mom playing the piano. Even though I was just a little boy, I could sense the anointing on them as they sang. That was about fifty-eight years ago, but right now as I think about it I've got what we used to call, "Holy Ghost goose bumps," running up and down my arms.

As the church began to grow, Mom felt a need to start what used to be called, "The Women's Auxiliary." Today it's called, "The Women's Ministries." As a result the church began to really grow and reach out to other women within a five to ten mile radius of the church. In two years we went from fifteen to about seventy in church attendance. Most of those people have now joined Mom and Dad in Heaven, but the memories of them are still precious to me. Mitchell and Emily Walker were among some of the first ones to get saved and join the church. I remember Mom telling about the Sunday Emily got saved. Mitchell and Emily had two children. Carolyn was the oldest and Tommy was their baby. Susan came along a little bit later. On the Sunday Emily got saved, she and Mitchell were both so under conviction they could hardly stand it. Emily was the first to step out and go to the Altar. I don't know if she was aware that Mitchell wanted to go to the Altar or not, but somebody had to stay with the children. They say he was mad the whole week, but the following Sunday he got saved. Mitchell has gone to be with the Lord now. Emily is still with us and I don't think she's changed one bit. I called her as I was writing this to make sure I remembered everything correctly.

After Dad's ministry at the Bethel Church was completed, we moved to the North Henderson Pentecostal Holiness Church in Henderson, North Carolina. Mom taught the Adult Bible Class there. The North Henderson Church was different from most churches in that there would be a larger crowd for Sunday School than there would be for the morning worship service. In most churches it's the opposite.

On this particular Sunday, Mom was teaching on the Apostle Paul. Sitting in her class was Butch and Janice Jones. Butch was a big man and I don't mean fat either. He was very muscular. If there was going to be a confrontation, you definitely wanted Butch on your side. Mom finished her lesson and dismissed the class, and as usual many left. Mom didn't know it at the time but God used that lesson in a mighty way. Butch and Janice went home and when time came to eat lunch, Butch couldn't eat. He just sat and cried.

He couldn't sleep that night. The next morning He went to work, but had to come home. On Tuesday he didn't go to work. On Wednesday he went to the doctor and told the doctor he couldn't sleep or eat. He just sat there and cried. The doctor asked him when this all started and he said, "Sunday morning at church." The doctor said, "I can give you something to help you sleep, but I really believe you need to talk to your pastor." When they returned home, they called Mom and Dad and asked them to come to their house. When Butch told them what had happened they started praying with him, and then Dad said, "Butch, prayer meeting starts in just a little while. Why don't you come to church?" Well, he did and the Lord saved him. Butch went to be with the Lord in 1989. As I was writing this I wanted to make sure I remembered everything correctly, so I called Janice and she confirmed everything. She said, "Your mother is the reason Butch is in heaven today."

In 1963 we moved to Gretna, Virginia. I lived there until I went in the Army in 1968. One funny thing that I remember happened when we were living in Gretna. Mom was fussing at me for something I had said or done, which was not a rare thing. I was about eighteen years old at the time and a lot of people say I was very mischievous. Can you imagine such a thing? We were in the kitchen and Mom was just letting me have it. I walked over to her, picked her up in my arms, and gently set her in the kitchen sink. I can see her legs hanging over the side of the sink now. "You had better get me out of this sink right now. I'm going to give you the worst whopping you ever had in your life." I very calmly leaned up against the wall and folded my arms in front of me and said, "Mama, if you promise not to whop me I'll get you out." (A whopping is much worse than a whipping, in case you didn't know.) "I'm not promising you anything but a good whopping." I sat down in a chair and just looked at her. When she started laughing, I knew I was safe. She told that story many, many times and then she would laugh and say, "I don't know what in the world I'm going to do with that boy."

Mom would much rather do for others than she would for herself. Nice fancy things didn't mean much to her. I guess it's a good thing. Being a preacher's wife, and having to move as much as we did, things just didn't last very long. I remember her saying once, "Two moves are equal to one fire." It definitely took its toll on furniture, but I never heard her complain, not one time. This is how she felt about my Dad's ministry. "When we got married we became one. When God called him to preach my job was to be right there helping any way I could." Mom taught Sunday School, played the piano, sang specials, was president of the Women's Auxiliary, worked and prayed around the altar with those seeking the Lord, and if Daddy was sick or out of town, she would preach. If I've ever seen what I thought was the perfect preacher's wife, it was my Mom.

While pastoring at the Mt. Calvary Pentecostal Holiness Church, my dad received a phone call one day from a couple who were missionaries and they were raising their support to go back to the mission field. They wanted to know if they could come speak at the church. Mom and dad had a tender spot in their hearts for missions and of course said yes even though they didn't know them personally. After the service that Sunday morning, Mom and the lady were in the kitchen getting lunch prepared. Dad and the husband were in the living room talking. When the lady realized that Mom and Dad had gone to Holmes Bible College she began asking Mom questions. "Sister Jones, when you and Brother Jones were at Holmes, did you visit churches on weekends and show films about missions?" Mom said, "Yes we did." Then the lady asked," Do you remember going to a certain church for a service?" She gave some details about the church and the service that jogged Mom's memory, and Mom said, "Yes,

I remember there was one little girl that came to the altar and said the Lord had called her to be a missionary." The Lady replied, "That was me. I knew I had seen you somewhere before."

I have thought several times my book was complete. That was about five stories ago. I had decided not to write a story specifically about Mom because she is mentioned so much throughout my book. I was trying to avoid being any more repetitious than I already have been, but so many things keep coming to my mind. I feel all these things need to be told because I want my daughter, Angel, my nieces Anna and Shawn and my nephew, Doug, to have a written record about their grandmother. She was a very special lady.

There's one final thought I would like to leave with you. In December of 1968 when I was in the Army I flew home from California. I had not been home since I was drafted and I was so much looking forward to coming home for Christmas. I flew from San Francisco to Dulles International Airport in Washington D. C. When we landed, the jet didn't taxi to the terminal like they do at most airports. We stopped on the tarmac several hundred yards away from the terminal and a large mobile lounge drove out to the plane. It looked like a large waiting room on wheels with couches, and it had windows on each side. At each end was a door that looked like an elevator door. When it reached the plane it raised up until it was level with the door of the plane. When the door opened we walked in and it drove us back to the terminal. When we reached the terminal it plugged right into the wall and the doors opened. I was hoping to be among the first to get off, but as it turned out I was among the last. I remember trying to look over everyone's head to see if I could see my Mom and Dad. All of a sudden I saw a little grey headed lady doing the very same thing. She was standing on her tip toes looking for me. When she saw me the biggest smile came across her face. When she got to me she grabbed me, hugged me, kissed me, and held onto me just as tight as she could. Then I saw my Daddy. He grabbed me and gave me a big ole hug and said, "Welcome home son". If that moment could have lasted forever, it would have been OK with me.

I've thought about that precious memory so many times, and then one day it dawned on me. It's going to happen again. I don't know exactly how it's going to take place, but I try to imagine those gates of pearl swinging open and there standing before me are my Mom and Dad to welcome me home.

First Corinthians 2:9 reads, *"But as it is written, Eye hath not seen, nor ear heard, neither have entered into the heart of man, the things which God hath prepared for them that love Him."*

That's one reunion I don't want to miss. If we miss Heaven, we've missed everything!

SUMMARY

My hope is that this book has been a blessing to you as well as entertaining. Over the past year or so I've probably used a box of tissues wiping tears from my eyes as well as from my keyboard. I've also done a lot of laughing. I guess it would be safe to say I've experienced every emotion known to mankind during the process of writing this book. I've learned a lot about myself and I've done a lot of growing as a person. I've learned that in the past I've probably been harder on myself in some ways than I should have been and then I guess in other ways I may have been too easy. I do feel that we should set high standards for ourselves, but at the same time we shouldn't beat ourselves up if we fall short.

I want to thank my wife for her help in making this book possible. I did all the typing, but she did most of the editing and proof reading. Someone asked the question, "Are all these stories true?" The answer is, "Yes, they are. I did not make any of them up. They really did happen." When possible I called someone to verify the details and to make sure my memory served me well.

If you have a comment or a question I would love to hear from you. If you accepted the Lord as your Savior as a result of reading this book, or if it helped you in some way, or if you would like to order more books you are welcome to contact me at:

billyihavebeensaved@gmail.com

God bless you is my prayer!

CPSIA information can be obtained at www.ICGtesting.com
Printed in the USA
269792BV00002B/5/P